PATRONAGE AND POWER
IN THE MEDIEVAL
WELSH MARCH

PATRONAGE AND POWER IN THE MEDIEVAL WELSH MARCH

One Family's Story

David Stephenson

UNIVERSITY OF WALES PRESS
2021

www.uwp.co.uk

British Library Cataloguing-in-Publication Data
A catalogue record for this book is available from the British Library.

ISBN: 978-1-78683-818-6
e-ISBN: 978-1-78683-819-3

The publisher acknowledges the financial assistance of the Books Council of Wales.

MIX
Paper from
responsible sources
FSC® C013604

Typeset by Marie Doherty
Printed by CPI Antony Rowe, Melksham, United Kingdom

For Jan

Contents

Preface   ix
Acknowledgements   xiii
Genealogical Chart   xv
Map   xvii

Prologue: Crisis at Cefnllys   1

Chapter 1:   Hywel ap Meurig: Questions of Ancestry   5
Chapter 2:   Diligence, Danger and Distinction: The Career   11
              of Hywel ap Meurig

              Intermezzo: The Sons of Hywel ap Meurig   26

Chapter 3:   Philip ap Hywel: Administrative Eminence and   33
              Political Peril
Chapter 4:   The Empire Builders: Master Rees ap Hywel and   51
              His Sons
Chapter 5:   Continuity and New Directions: The Career   69
              of Sir Philip Clanvowe
Chapter 6:   The Last of the Line: The Later Clanvowes   81
Chapter 7:   Some Reflections   109

Appendix: Meurig and William, Sons of Rees ap Meurig   123

Bibliography   129
Index   137

Preface

The family which is the subject of this book emerged into the light of historical sources in the March of Wales during the thirteenth century. The March of Wales (*Marchia Wallie*) was a term used in the medieval period to describe the lands, of varying extent from place to place and from time to time, which lay to the west of the English mid-land counties or which ran along the southern coastal rim of Wales. Historians have argued over the date or dates of its creation but have generally agreed that it was a land of Anglo-Norman, subsequently English, lords who exercised quasi-regal powers over a Welsh population who were often confined to the upland areas of lordships, the 'Welshries', and an immigrant English population who inhabited the more fertile lowlands and the towns which were created and privileged by the lords.

In that reconstruction of the March the Welsh population is often pictured as being of little account, the principal focus being on the Marcher lords themselves.[1] And yet that was not always true, and it became less true as the thirteenth century wore on. In many areas of the March English 'gentry', often lesser lords holding sub-lordships or manors, were joined by a growing elite of Welsh notables who can also be described as gentry. Writing in a celebrated study of the fourteenth-century March of Wales published in 1978, Rees Davies noted that 'the "gentry" of the medieval March are an even more elusive group than their English equivalents. Much may yet be achieved by studies of individual families….'[2] The present book is one such study. I cannot claim Rees Davies's words as an inspiration: if I read them, many years ago, I had either forgotten them or they did not make the impression which they should have done. But stumbling upon them when this book was being finished, they seem to be a kind of justification.

Not that the attempt to recount the story of the family that dominates these pages needs much by way of justification. Emerging in historical documents as a Welsh family of relatively modest status on the western fringe of Herefordshire in the early thirteenth century they rose to great heights of power and influence not only in the March but in the land known as *pura Wallia*, 'pure Wales', to the west. Here they attained the very highest positions: in the fourteenth century a member of the family was the first Welshman to hold the office of Justiciar of South Wales, while he and one of his sons and a nephew acted as deputy Justiciars. By virtue of specific royal commissions, the family periodically exercised a remarkable control over much of Wales. And some of them would climb even higher, as they turned eastwards from Wales and the March.

Until both main branches of the family died out as a result of failure of heirs in the male line, they had succeeded in surviving for nearly two centuries in very turbulent times. They were deeply involved in some of the most dramatic events of the Middle Ages in Wales and England such as the fall of Llywelyn, Prince of Wales, and the struggles of Edward II and his barons which ultimately led to the capture and death of the king. The family produced at least one literary figure, a member of Geoffrey Chaucer's circle, as well as soldiers, diplomats, powerful administrators, persons of note at the far from tranquil court of King Richard II; two attained the somewhat hazardous status of Welsh Marcher lords; another was a prominent crusader, while yet another fought against Owain Glyn Dŵr, was captured by his forces, and subsequently freed. In addition, though some members of the family were dignitaries of the Church, others were suspected of the heresy of Lollardy.

And beyond involvement in war, rebellion, and suspected heresy, the family had to face the problems of the Great Famine of the second decade of the fourteenth century, the Black Death of the late 1340s and the return of plague at intervals after that date. Merely to have survived as long as they did is an achievement. Some individual members of the family have attracted attention from historians, but this is the first time that a tolerably full account of the descendants of an obscure

Welshman named Meurig ap Philip has been given. At first sight the task of tracing the family's progress seems a more than daunting one: record repositories have so far failed to reveal an archive of family documents; chronicle references to the family are far from plentiful, even if sometimes telling; no Welsh poetry survives by which we may gauge their impact within the Welsh communities of the March and southern Wales – though some of the Welsh poets showed themselves ready to compose praise poems for the 'English' lords of the March and for the Welsh gentry figures who acted as powerful agents of royal and Marcher rule in Wales. But enough scattered material survives to make possible a portrait of the several generations whose experiences and achievements mark them out as amongst the most interesting and significant families of Welsh origin in the medieval March. They cannot meaningfully be described as 'typical' of a class of rising gentry in the March; in those lands, above the level of those who struggled simply to survive through warfare, political turmoil, deteriorating weather conditions, famine and plague, it is close to pointless to label men and women as 'typical'. Their shared characteristics were ambition, opportunism and tenacity. How those characteristics manifested themselves in individual cases was often the product of a great diversity of backgrounds and circumstances, that mysterious chemistry that makes the study of the medieval March so fascinating.

Notes

[1] See, for example, Brock Holden, *Lords of the Central Marches*: *English Aristocracy and Frontier Society 1087–1265* (Oxford: Oxford University Press, 2008), where the Welsh make few appearances. The works of Max Lieberman, *The March of Wales 1067–1300* (Cardiff: University of Wales Press, 2008), and *idem*, *The Medieval March of Wales: The Creation and Perception of a Frontier, 1066–1283* (Cambridge: Cambridge University Press, 2010) are marked by a more balanced approach.
[2] R. R. Davies, *Lordship and Society in the March of Wales, 1282–1400* (Oxford: The Clarendon Press, 1978), p. 423.

Acknowledgements

This book has had a complex gestation. Members of my Medieval History classes first suggested that I should work up my interest in Hywel ap Meurig and his family into a book, while exploring the problems and opportunities presented by working on a micro-narrative. I began to investigate the terrain associated with the rise of Hywel and his family, but my intention to present this at the annual Medieval History late-summer trip in 2018 was put in jeopardy when I was unable to accompany the tour. My thanks are due to Stella and Charles Gratrix, who stood in for me, and led the members around parts of the central March of Wales, like the castles at Builth and Bronllys, which had significant if then largely unacknowledged connections with that family. Stella furthered interest in Hywel by encouraging in inimitable fashion the chanting of his name at key locations. After that, I felt I had little choice but to get this fascinating family story into print. That, in turn, gave rise to further obligations: my thanks are due to key members of the staff at University of Wales Press, to Llion Wigley for his interest in the project and his faith in the book; to Dafydd Jones in editorial, and all those involved in the production process, especially Heather Palomino for her sensitive copy-editing and Marie Doherty for her expert typesetting. The publication of the book was greatly facilitated by a grant from the Books Council of Wales, for which I am most grateful. One further obligation must be recorded: writing took place in sometimes challenging circumstances, and I am much indebted to my wife Jan for her tolerance and interest.

Such diverse encouragement and support has been crucial in the conception and completion of this volume.

Genealogical Chart

Genealogy of the descendants of Meurig ap Philip

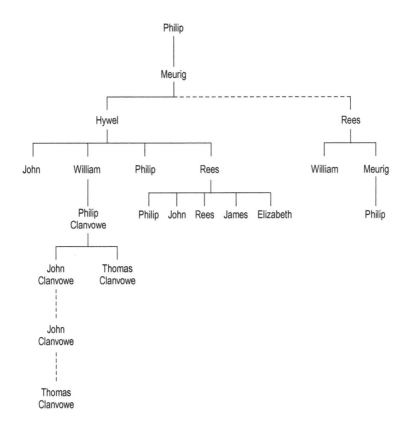

Map

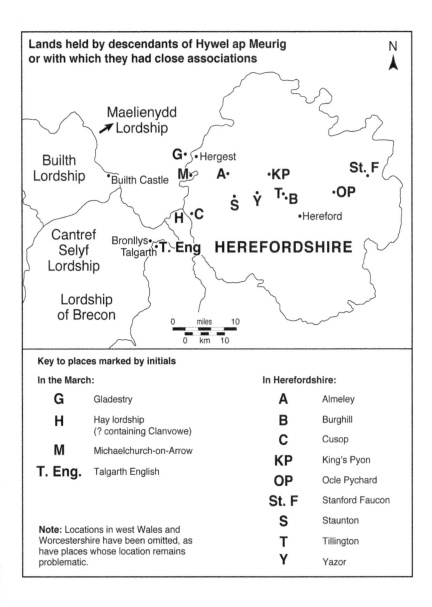

Lands held by descendants of Hywel ap Meurig or with which they had close associations

N

Maelienydd Lordship

Builth Lordship

•Builth Castle

G• •Hergest

M• A• •KP St. F

Ṡ Ẏ T•·B •OP

H •C

•Hereford

Cantref Selyf Lordship

Bronllys• ·T. Eng
Talgarth

HEREFORDSHIRE

Lordship of Brecon

0 miles 10

0 km 10

Key to places marked by initials

In the March:

G	Gladestry
H	Hay lordship (? containing Clanvowe)
M	Michaelchurch-on-Arrow
T. Eng.	Talgarth English

Note: Locations in west Wales and Worcestershire have been omitted, as have places whose location remains problematic.

In Herefordshire:

A	Almeley
B	Burghill
C	Cusop
KP	King's Pyon
OP	Ocle Pychard
St. F	Stanford Faucon
S	Staunton
T	Tillington
Y	Yazor

Prologue:
Crisis at Cefnllys

In the summer of 1258, the kingdom of England was in turmoil. Political tensions between Henry III of England and his leading barons exploded into a real crisis. Exasperated by their effective exclusion from the king's government, the barons forced Henry to accept a Council of Twenty-Four, half to be chosen by the king and half by the baronial opposition. That council would begin the process of reforming Henry's government. Thus began years of confrontation between king and baronage, much of it violent, which threatened to tear England apart. This crisis had wide-reaching effects, nowhere more so than in Wales. As so often, problems within England created an opportunity for an ambitious Welsh ruler. This time, that ruler was Llywelyn ap Gruffudd, prince of Gwynedd. Taking advantage of the distraction of the king and his barons Llywelyn was able to conquer or bring to his side much of Wales.

By 1262 Llywelyn had extended his power even into the Middle March, that area of the Anglo-Welsh borderland which would in later centuries become Radnorshire. Llywelyn's conquests in the March were aided by the fact that many of the magnates of that region were closely involved in the political struggles in England. Two of the greatest Marcher lords, Roger Mortimer of Wigmore and Humphrey de Bohun, earl of Hereford and lord of Brecon, had been baronial nominees on the Council of Twenty-Four, and they continued to be deeply involved in the politics of the English realm. They had limited time for involvement in the affairs of Wales. The Mortimer family had been fighting for over one hundred and sixty years to establish themselves as lords of the March and in the process had developed an obsessive determination to secure their hold on the great lordship of Maelienydd.[1] But now their hold on that land was under grave threat.

Describing developments in late November of 1262, a Welsh chronicler writing at the abbey of Cwmhir in central Wales told of dramatic events at the nearby castle of Cefnllys, which was the principal stronghold of the Mortimers in Maelienydd:

> In that year, on the eve of the feast of St Andrew (i.e. 29th November) the castle of Cefnllys was captured and destroyed by the efforts of the men of Maelienydd ... Then the Lord Roger (Mortimer) and Humphrey de Bohun Junior, together with the flower of the young men of the whole March entered the ruined walls of Cefnllys, with much equipment, aiming to repair the damage to the walls. Hearing this Lord Llywelyn ap Gruffudd, prince of Wales, bringing with him all the greater men of Wales came towards them and laid siege to them until, driven by starvation, they requested permission to leave, with their arms but not in hostile array, which was conceded to them by the pious prince, led by mercy. And so it was done.[2]

Another chronicler, this time writing at the abbey of Strata Florida in Ceredigion, added some significant details: he noted that Cefnllys had initially been taken by treachery by certain of the men of Maelienydd, who had called in the prince's officers. It was those officers who had burned and damaged the castle. And in another addition to the story, the Strata Florida chronicler had recorded that the men of Maelienydd who had taken the castle had killed the gatekeepers and had seized the constable of the castle, together with his wife and his sons and daughters. These had evidently not been killed but had been taken as prisoners: 'and when Roger (Mortimer) heard that he came with many leading men as his supporters in arms. And he stayed within the castle walls for a few days. And the Lord Llywelyn's officers made that known to him. And he gathered a host and came to Maelienydd, and he received the homage of the men of the land and took two other castles; and he gave Roger and his men leave to return.' It had been a dramatic incident. And the account of the Strata Florida chronicler includes one further and crucial detail about the castellan who had been captured with his family when Cefnllys was taken. His name was Hywel ap Meurig.[3]

Notes

1   A convenient summary is provided by Charles Hopkinson and Martin Speight, *The Mortimers, Lords of the March* (Almeley: Logaston Press, 2002).
2   J. Williams ab Ithel (ed.), *Annales Cambriae* (London: Rolls Series, 1860), p. 100 (my translation). The text (the Breviate text of *Annales Cambriae*) is now better consulted in the far superior edition of Henry Gough-Cooper in the website of the Welsh Chronicles Research Group at *http://croniclau. bangor.ac.uk/documents/AC%20B%20first%20edition.pdf* (accessed 22 July 2020). For the nearby location of the chronicler, see David Stephenson, 'The Chronicler of Cwm-hir Abbey, 1257–63: The Construction of a Welsh Chronicle', in R. A. Griffiths and P. R. Schofield (eds), *Wales and the Welsh in the Middle Ages* (Cardiff: University of Wales Press, 2011), pp. 29–45.
3   Thomas Jones (ed. and trans.), *Brut y Tywysogyon, or the Chronicle of the Princes: Peniarth MS. 20 Version* (henceforth *BT Pen20*) (Cardiff: University of Wales Press, 1952), p. 112.

Hywel ap Meurig:
Questions of Ancestry

Hywel ap Meurig's very name was of significance. In the first place, the patronymic 'ap' ('son of'), reveals quite clearly that he was Welsh. This was no English official of an English Marcher lord. Indeed, the Marcher lord in question, Roger Mortimer, was himself half-Welsh, for his mother was Gwladus Ddu (the dark-haired, dark-eyed), one of the daughters of Llywelyn ap Gruffudd's grandfather, Llywelyn ab Iorwerth (Llywelyn the Great).[1] So Roger Mortimer and Prince Llywelyn were cousins. Roger's Welsh ancestry may make it more intelligible that he had employed a Welshman in a particularly powerful and sensitive post, as castellan of the most significant Mortimer castle in Wales yet built. For the castle of Cefnllys was a stone castle, built relatively recently, by Roger Mortimer's father, Ralph, in 1242.[2] By the middle decades of the thirteenth century it is possible to discern within the Marcher lordships a rising class of Welsh officials. The Marcher lords were becoming more prepared to entrust important and sensitive posts to Welsh magnates who were happy to act as their leading officials, and to increase their own status and influence in the process.[3] It is clear that Hywel ap Meurig was an early member of this class.

Hywel ap Meurig's name also reveals him as a man already known in a rather different context. As early as 1259, even before we have clear evidence that he was a leading official of a lord such as Roger Mortimer, he appears as a royal appointee engaged with others of Henry III's officers in negotiations with none other than Llywelyn ap Gruffudd.[4] Ironically, by the summer of 1262 Hywel was one of the officials charged with extending a truce with the prince and dealing with Llywelyn's claim that the previous truce had been broken by, amongst others, Roger Mortimer.[5] It is probably the result of his record as a royal officer, and the fact that he was high in the service of Roger Mortimer, that explains why Hywel and his family were not killed in the seizure of Cefnllys. They were worth money in the form of ransom payments if they were kept alive. It therefore comes as no surprise that we find Hywel ap Meurig released and at liberty within months of his capture.[6] He and his family had presumably been bought out of captivity.

All of this raises the question: who exactly was this Hywel ap Meurig? How had he come to be so prominent, both in royal service and in that of one of the greatest of the Marcher lords? At some point, far in the future, a member of Hywel's family would have a genealogy drawn up which revealed his ancestry and of course that of his descendants. The genealogy is a revelation. It shows that Hywel was the son of Meurig, who in turn was the son of Rhys, whose father was Philip, son of Rhys Mechyll.[7] This is the point at which the lineage becomes really interesting, for Rhys Mechyll was a Welsh ruler, a son of Rhys Gryg, lord of the great castle of Dinefwr and ruler of a realm which covered the Tywi Valley.[8] Rhys Gryg was perhaps the most illustrious son of the Lord Rhys, the prince of South Wales and one of the most powerful Welsh rulers of the twelfth century. The genealogy thus shows clearly the background to the prominence of Hywel ap Meurig: his pedigree as a descendant of Welsh rulers appears impeccable. There is only one problem: the pedigree was demonstrably fictitious.

The problem can be set out very briefly. Rhys Mechyll died in 1244.[9] Hywel ap Meurig died in 1281, only thirty-seven years, little more than a generation, after the death of the man recorded in his genealogy as his great-great-grandfather.[10] This is in itself highly unlikely, the more so as Hywel ap Meurig was clearly no mere youth when he acted as a negotiator for Henry III and a castellan for Roger Mortimer in the period 1259–62. We may therefore assume his birth took place several years before the death of his alleged great-great-grandfather, who had in turn died relatively young, a mere ten years after *his* father. The genealogy creates a clearly absurd situation. The pedigree-maker responsible for constructing the genealogy of Hywel al Meurig was quite probably commissioned by the family to provide them with a particularly distinguished ancestry consonant with what we shall see were their significant worldly achievements. But we do not have to be reliant on his work, for there is an alternative, much more credible, and significantly different account of Hywel's forebears and descendants.

This exists in an official government record of the fourteenth century, an inquisition, or formal enquiry, ordered by the royal government. The record of the enquiry tells us in detail about one branch of Hywel's descendants, and about some of his ancestors. The enquiry took place before two royal appointees, Adam Lucas and John de Mershton, in the presence of Ieuan ap Rhys, acting as deputy for the keeper of the manor of Radnor, Hugh Tyrel, whose absence may have been the result of embarrassment, as the record suggests. It was taken at Weobley, in Herefordshire, in June 1339:

> Philip de Clanvowe and his ancestors have been reeves in fee of the land of *Glaudestre* [Gladestry], an appurtenance of the manor of Radnor, receiving yearly from that manor seven ells of cloth worth five marks a cloth, which the said Philip had from Margaret Mortimer in her time. Philip ap Hywel, his uncle, whose heir he is, had the same from Edmund Mortimer in his time, and from Maud his mother in her time. Hywel ap Meurig, father of the said Philip ap Hywel and grandfather of the said Philip de Clanvowe, whose heir he is, had the same from the said Maud in her time. Meurig ap Philip, father of the said Hywel, had the same from William de Braose in his time. And so the said Philip de Clanvowe and his ancestors had the same from time beyond memory until the manor came to the king's hand by the death of Margaret Mortimer by reason of the minority of Roger, son and heir of Edmund Mortimer. The cloth is in arrears for the whole time of Hugh Tyrel as keeper of the manor.[11]

So here we have a line of Hywel's immediate forebears running Hywel ap Meurig ap Philip … Luckily the existence of Meurig ap Philip, Hywel's father as alleged in the 1339 Inquisition, can be confirmed from a number of sources. In 1241 the head of the Mortimer family, Ralph, was engaged in a sharp struggle, effectively a regional war, to re-establish the Mortimer possessions in central Wales after they had been driven out by Llywelyn the Great and the local Welsh dynasty descended from Cadwallon ap Madog, in the years after 1214. Several charters in which Welsh lords of the commote of Gwerthrynion formally relinquished their lordship in that territory to Ralph Mortimer after the conflict of 1241 contain the name of Meurig ap Philip among the witnesses.[12] It therefore appears that Meurig was amongst the Welsh magnates of the Middle March who accepted Mortimer lordship and who formed part of the entourage of a Mortimer lord, particularly after control of Radnor lordship passed from the de Braose family to the Mortimers in 1230. When the name of Meurig ap Philip occurs in the witness lists to these charters, it comes towards the tail-end of the lists, suggesting that though worthy of inclusion among the named witnesses, Meurig was not an official, or indeed a tenant, of the first rank.[13] That supposition conforms well to the evidence that Meurig had acted as the reeve of Gladestry in the period of de Braose lordship, for the reeve was effectively a manorial official and not normally a magnate.[14]

But a rather different impression is gained from an earlier record. This relates to events in 1216, when King John was struggling to shore up his regime against both baronial opposition and an invasion of England mounted by the French king's son Louis. By late July he was moving through the Welsh March in the hope of raising support there. In the Middle March he could hope for some help from the loyal Hugh Mortimer, but the Mortimers' position in the region had recently suffered a heavy blow when they were pushed out of Maelienydd. The Braose family, once so dominant in the region, had been alienated by John's breaking of William de Braose after 1208 and the death in a royal prison of his wife Matilda and their son William in 1210.[15] With the power of the lords of the Middle March in abeyance, John evidently decided to appeal to the Welsh notables of the region. This is the background to a letter which he dispatched from Hay on 28 July, calling to his aid a number of Welsh leaders, who were assured that a meeting with the king was going to be to their benefit and that they would have safe conduct coming to, staying with, and going from the king. Those summoned included Hywel ap Philip and his brother Meurig.[16] That this Meurig ap Philip is to be identified as the father of Hywel ap Meurig is strongly suggested by the name of Meurig's brother, Hywel. It seems likely that Meurig named his son after his brother. In John's letter Hywel and Meurig, sons of Philip are named second and third respectively in the list of those called to meet with the king. This seems to suggest a significantly higher status than that suggested by the Gwerthrynion charters. It is possible to reconcile these apparently varying estimations of Meurig ap Philip's status by suggesting that in 1241 it was his standing in the mixed English and Welsh Mortimer entourage which is reflected in his place in the witness lists, whereas in 1216 it was his place in the predominantly Welsh community to which John was appealing, that explains his prominence.

The background to Hywel ap Meurig's career thus appears to be that of a family well known in the Middle March and considered to be prominent in the Welsh community of the region without ever becoming important members of the courts and entourages of the leading Marcher lords, whose interests they apparently served. Hywel was thus above the level of most Welshmen of the March, who had little access to the English lords of the region, but his family background hardly marked him out for a career which would bring him great renown.

Notes

1   Hopkinson and Speight, *The Mortimers*, p. xii.
2   *BT Pen20*, p. 106.
3   See David Stephenson, *Medieval Wales c.1050–1332: Centuries of Ambiguity* (Cardiff: University of Wales Press, 2019), pp. 77–82.
4   See below, p. 12 and p. 28 n.3.
5   *Close Rolls, 1261–64*, p. 136.
6   See below, p. 13.
7   P. C. Bartrum, *Welsh Genealogies AD 300–1400* (Cardiff: University of Wales Press, 1974), III, p. 801 (Rhys ap Tewdwr 26). Much of this genealogy is problematic.
8   See Stephenson, *Medieval Wales*, pp. xxiv, 73.
9   *BT Pen20*, p. 106.
10 *Calendar of Close Rolls, 1279–88*, p. 142.
11 *Calendar of Inquisitions Miscellaneous, II (1308–48)*, p. 404 no. 1643.
12 For these documents, see J. Beverley Smith, 'The Middle March in the Thirteenth century', *Bulletin of the Board of Celtic Studies*, 24 (1970), 77–94, at pp. 89–93.
13 The place of Meurig ap Philip in the relevant witness lists is as follows (the numbering is editorial): no. 2: 10/11 (where Henrico filio Philippi is surely an error for Meurico filio Philippi); no. 3: 15/18; no. 4: 10/11;

no. 6: 10/11; no. 7:10/11; no. 8: 9/10 (where again Henrico filio Philippi is clearly a copyist's error for Meurico filio Philippi, the 'n' of Henrico and the 'u' of Meurico being effectively identical); no. 13: 10/11(and once more Henrico filio Philippi = Meurico filio Philippi). The very similar order of the witnesses' names in the various charters noticed here strongly suggests a perception of the relative seniority of the bearers.

14   The presence of Welshmen amongst witnesses to the acts of Marcher lords, becoming rather more common in the second quarter of the thirteenth century, had been, unusually, a feature of Mortimer governance a generation before that. The charter of Roger Mortimer to Cwmhir abbey in 1199, effectively a re-foundation charter, had several Welsh witnesses: see B. G. Charles, 'An early charter of the abbey of Cwmhir', *Radnorshire Society Transactions*, 40 (1970), 68–74.

15   *BT Pen 20*, p. 84.

16   Thomas Duffus Hardy (ed.), *Rotuli Litterarum Patentium in Turri Londinensi Asservati* vol. 1, part 1 [1201–1216] (London: Record Commission, 1835), p. 191.

2

Diligence, Danger and Distinction: The Career of Hywel ap Meurig

i. The entry into royal service

Hywel ap Meurig's father was clearly associated with the Mortimer family, the Marcher lords whose main residence was at Wigmore. In the charters by which Ralph Mortimer secured control of Maelienydd and Gwerthrynion after 1241 the name of Meurig ap Philip occurs towards the end of the witness lists. In the same lists there occur several more Mortimer associates. These include, significantly higher in the lists than Meurig, the names of John de Lingayne and Philip le Bret, always in that order. John de Lingayne's name marks him out as a member of the de Lingen family, Mortimer tenants, whose manor and castle lie just a few miles to the west of Wigmore. In a charter which was issued at some point in or after 1246, the abbot of Cwmhir granted to Roger, the successor of Ralph Mortimer, the right to make enclosures for hunting in the abbey woods. In this document the name of John de Lingayne appears in the witness list, following the names of regional magnates like Thomas Corbet (of Caus Castle on the Long Mountain), and Brian de Brompton, whose extensive lands in several counties were held of the Mortimers;[1] this time, however, the name of Meurig ap Philip is missing, and instead the charter is witnessed by his son, Hywel ap Meurig.[2] This appears to be the first record of Hywel's involvement in the Mortimer lordships, and shows that already he was mixing with men of regional prominence.

By the early 1260s Hywel was clearly a trusted administrator and military leader in the service of Roger Mortimer. We have already seen that in 1262 he held the important and – as events were to prove – dangerous post of castellan of Roger Mortimer's castle of Cefnllys. But another dimension of Hywel's career had become visible by the later 1250s, and this was his involvement in the diplomatic negotiations of Henry III with Llywelyn ap Gruffudd, increasingly the dominant force in Welsh politics. From 1259 onwards, Hywel was a frequent member of the teams of *dictatores* or arbiters who were deputed by Henry III to meet with the representatives of Llywelyn ap Gruffudd and prolong truces or settle problems regarding the implementation and maintenance of truces.[3]

What is particularly interesting about the lists of *dictatores* is that they generally contain, as well as Hywel's name, the names of John de Lingayne and Philip le Bret. The early lists contain what seems to be an erroneous name for Hywel: Ewen, or Owen ap Meurig.[4] There can be little doubt from the context – the association with John de Lingayne and Philip le Bret – that it is Hywel ap Meurig who is meant. But the error suggests that at this stage Hywel was new in royal service, and that his name was not known to the chancery clerks who were drawing up the copies of the letters which named the arbitrators. But his inclusion with John and Philip suggests that like them he was a Mortimer associate who had been seconded to royal service, possibly because of local knowledge and contacts which would be useful in determining issues arising in the March. There is plenty of evidence which suggests that at times the distinction between service to a Marcher lord and service to the king was not at all clear. The link with Roger Mortimer is made evident by a reference in 1260 to the fact that some of the letters empowering the arbitrators to act had been sent to the sheriffs of Shropshire and Staffordshire, those in favour of John de Lingayne, Hywel ap Meurig and Philip le Bret (in that order) had been passed to Roger Mortimer.[5]

It is also notable that the placing of Hywel's name, while low in the list of arbitrators, shows that he was keeping some exalted company. As well as John de Lingayne and Philip le Bret, who tend to head the lists, there was Hywel ap Madog, son of Madog ap Gruffudd (d. 1236) the lord of northern Powys, and Tudur ab Ednyfed, son of the celebrated Ednyfed Fychan, *distain* or steward (chief minister) of Llywelyn the Great who was effectively prince of most of Wales until his death in 1240.[6] Tudur spent time in England as a diplomatic hostage, and evidently became sufficiently anglicised to be employed as a royal negotiator with Llywelyn ap Gruffudd.[7] When he appears as an arbitrator, his brother Goronwy had succeeded to the office of *distain* and was in turn to be succeeded by Tudur himself in 1268.[8] The eminence of his fellow arbitrators is a clear indication that by the early 1260s Hywel ap Meurig was on the verge of becoming an influential figure.

Hywel may well have counted himself lucky that he and his family had survived the capture of Cefnllys in 1262. His prominence in royal service may have helped to protect him. But he was probably unaware that the spectacular phases of his career were yet to come.

ii. The lost years

One of the strangest things about the life of Hywel ap Meurig is that after he appears to have established himself in the service of both Roger Mortimer, one of the greatest of the Marcher lords of the thirteenth century, and King Henry III, he vanishes from our sight for some years. In the aftermath of the dramatic events at Cefnllys in November 1262 Hywel reappears in February 1263 as one of a group of men from Mortimer territory who are given protection – that is to say do not have to appear in court to answer charges – until Michaelmas of that year or for the duration of the war in Wales within that period.[9]

After that grant, Hywel does not come into view until the second half of 1271. The mystery of his disappearance from the records has no certain explanation. But we can perhaps make some educated guesses about its cause. In the first place it is worth noting that the list of February 1263 is headed by Roger Mortimer himself. It is thus a roll-call of the Mortimer affinity in the March. The fifth name on the list is that of Hywel's companion in the truce negotiations with Prince Llywelyn's representatives, John de Lingayne; Hywel's name is listed twenty-seventh out of a total of thirty-six names. This suggests either that Hywel had had a relatively lowly role in the truce negotiations – such as that of an interpreter – or that his prominence in the Mortimer hierarchy had declined following the capture of Cefnllys. It is possible therefore that Hywel had never been of great importance in the Welsh possessions of the Mortimer family, or that he had been held in some degree responsible for the loss of the castle of Cefnllys. But there are more telling factors to consider.

In the course of 1263 and the following two years the political order in England had fallen increasingly under the influence of Simon de Montfort, earl of Leicester, who had started as a reformer of the structure and the processes of government. After the battle of Lewes in 1264, and until the battle of Evesham in 1265, de Montfort controlled the government of much of England, holding the king himself as a captive, a mere puppet ruler.[10] As Roger Mortimer was a royalist stalwart, captured at Lewes and freed only by de Montfort's good grace, he and all of his affinity found no place in the governance of England, and so the absence of any of them from the records of the government is to be expected.

And we can go still further in explaining why Hywel ap Meurig does not appear in royal records in the years after 1263. When he does appear it is in Cantref Selyf in northern Brecon, over which the de Bohun earls of Hereford claimed overlordship.[11] By 1277 Hywel was described in a government record as the steward of the king, of Roger Mortimer and of Humphrey de Bohun.[12] These two families had not always been allies, but in 1263 de Bohun's grandfather had moved from the baronial opposition to join Roger Mortimer in support for the king. When the grandson succeeded to the earldom in 1275, he was increasingly aligned with Mortimer in challenging the power of Prince Llywelyn. It is possible therefore to picture Hywel ap Meurig as one of the men who had helped to establish and maintain a working relationship between these two great Marcher dynasties, de Bohun and Mortimer. Such an involvement in the complex politics of the Middle March is unlikely to have shown up in the formal governmental records of the years after 1263.

Finally, it is also possible that Hywel's absence from much of the official documentation of the time may reflect the probability that he was engaged in this period in providing himself with a new base for his activities. We shall see that in later years one of his sons was resident in Hergest at the house from which Hergest Court developed, very close to the border between Herefordshire and the March, and within a short

distance of Gladestry, a place in which the family had been prominent as hereditary reeves for generations.[13] The house at Hergest Court
survives and is generally described as a later medieval structure.[14] But
one of the internal timbers has been dendrochronologically dated to
1267 – and this raises the strong suspicion that the first house on the
site had been begun by Hywel ap Meurig, as a base close to the edge
of the March where his lord Roger Mortimer was so influential as an
opponent of the newly acknowledged prince of Wales.[15]

The above scenarios are of course matters of speculation, but they
are supported by the sparse facts that we have available to us, and it is
likely that they are all in some measure valuable in filling in the evi-
dential gaps of the years between early 1263 and the late summer of
1271. They do at least enable us to pick up the story of Hywel's life in
the latter year without too much difficulty.

iii. Bringing down a prince:
Hywel ap Meurig and Llywelyn ap Gruffudd

Hywel ap Meurig reappears in record sources in the late summer of
1271 in very interesting circumstances. He was prominent amongst
the witnesses to a charter issued by Meurig ap Gruffudd in favour of
Dore abbey.[16] The grant appears to have been made at the castle of
Bronllys, the caput of Cantref Selyf, the northern cantref of the lordship of Brecon. Cantref Selyf had been held by John Giffard in right
of his wife, Maud Clifford, heiress of the last of the Clifford lords of
that territory, who had died in 1263. The witness list is headed by
Walter de Traveley, a member of a family with a history of service to
the lords of Brecon. De Traveley is described as the constable and the
steward of Bronllys. Hywel ap Meurig witnesses second, immediately
after de Traveley.

The first thing that is of significance about this charter is that it was
issued in territory which according to the Treaty of Montgomery of
1267 should have been in the hands of Llywelyn ap Gruffudd, prince
of Wales. But the grant makes no mention of Llywelyn, and the witness list contains no one who can be identified as one of his officials.
Instead, it appears that the territory of Bronllys had been regained by

its previous lords, and thus removed from the possession of Prince Llywelyn. It is one of the first signs that Llywelyn's control of the principality which had been confirmed to him in 1267 was slipping.[17]

The identity of some of those present at the grant to Dore abbey is a second point of great significance. Walter de Traveley can be assumed to have had no loyalty to Prince Llywelyn,[18] but it is the record of the allegiances of some of the Welsh witnesses that is important. Hywel ap Meurig, as a partisan and official of Roger Mortimer was closely involved with a lord who was one of the prince's most consistent opponents. He had certainly suffered for his support for Mortimer when he was captured by the insurgents who took control of Cefnllys in 1262. And as we have seen he had a history of service to King Henry III. The third witness, Rhys ap Meurig, is surely to be identified as the man of that name who was the constable of Bronllys under the Clifford lord in the time before Llywelyn ap Gruffudd had occupied the lordship.[19] Also amongst the witnesses was one Llywelyn ap Caradog, who can be identified, as we shall see, as an opponent of Prince Llywelyn.[20] The names of other witnesses appear to reveal close association with the Clifford lords.[21] The man in whose name the charter was issued, Meurig ap Gruffudd, was going to be forced within four months of the grant to Dore to put up sureties in the sum of eighty marks to guarantee his future good conduct towards the prince.[22] He was clearly a man whose activities had placed him under suspicion of disloyalty to Llywelyn ap Gruffudd.

It appears, then, that the grant to Dore in August 1271 was the occasion for a gathering of men who were notionally subjects of the prince of Wales, but who were in fact working to erode his rule in the Middle March. The gathering at Bronllys looks very much like an indication of the growing resistance to Llywelyn amongst the Welsh community of the region. And Hywel ap Meurig was prominent amongst that resistance.

Over the following years it becomes clearer just how deeply involved Hywel was in the opposition to Llywelyn ap Gruffudd's regime in the Marchland. In the spring of 1274, he was clearly acting as a Mortimer agent, gathering information about Prince Llywelyn's intentions when he visited the borderland. At some time in late March of that year he wrote to Lady Maud Mortimer (Maud de Braose, wife of Roger

Mortimer) to inform her that he had heard that the prince would come to Cedewain to see his new castle (Dolforwyn). It had been stocked for three weeks at his cost, and in addition all of his bailiffs in Wales were to supply him with provisions, each for two days at their own cost. The prince had, Hywel reported, arranged for large amounts of beer and of mead to be brewed in advance of his arrival. Hywel had also heard that Llywelyn would then go into the forest of Clun to find a place for a new castle, and he noted that it was rumoured that a party of the great men of England were coming to meet him there. Whether that would be for good or evil Hywel did not know. He advised Lady Maud to send this news on to his lord, and also urged her to keep watch at Clun and everywhere so that they should be well prepared.[23]

This letter from Hywel to Lady Maud is of great significance. In the first instance it demonstrates how high in the service of the Mortimers Hywel stood by early 1274. He was clearly in a position to offer guidance to the wife of Roger Mortimer in the expectation that it would be followed. The quality of his intelligence was impressive. His comments on the arrangements which the prince had made for his stay at his new castle (Dolforwyn) give a valuable insight into the machinery of government within Llywelyn's principality, suggesting good communications between the prince and his local officials. It has been argued that the search for a new castle in the forest of Clun led to a partial rebuilding of Castell Bryn Amlwg in that area by Llywelyn ap Gruffudd, who was certainly in occupation of the Clun Welshry at that period.[24] Hywel's report of a rumour that some of the magnates of England were arranging to come and speak with Llywelyn, coming as it did at the time when the absent Edward I was about to return from Crusade and to go through the ceremony of coronation, is perhaps the best indication we have that there was a faction within the English nobility who were willing to come to an agreement with Llywelyn, presumably to stave off the expense – and hence taxation – of a major war. Most significant perhaps is the emphasis in Hywel's report on developments which might impact on Mortimer interests. His reference to the possibility that Llywelyn might build a new castle in the forest of Clun must be read in the light of the fact that the Clun Welshry – that is the forest – bordered the land of Maelienydd, where Roger Mortimer was maintaining a lordship that was constantly under threat from Llywelyn. Hywel's insistence that watch should be kept from Clun itself – where Roger Mortimer was custodian of the lordship in the minority of the FitzAlan heir – was clearly intended to ensure that developments in the Clun/Maelienydd region were taken seriously.[25]

That Hywel ap Meurig was present in 1271 in lands where lordship was being asserted by both Humphrey de Bohun as overlord and John Giffard as immediate lord suggest that he may already have been active in the interests of those magnates. But it is clear from the letter to Lady Maud in March 1274 that he also remained committed to the Mortimer cause. This did not, however, exhaust his interests or his ambition. In May of 1275 Hywel is found with a colleague, Henry de Bray, receiving a royal commission to survey the castles, lands and tenements of the royal counties of Carmarthen and Cardigan which were currently held by the king's brother Edmund, and to report on the state they were in with regard to armour and provisions.[26] The importance of the commission is two-fold: it brought Hywel into contact with Henry de Bray, a royal official who would feature in his life in the following years, and it established Hywel as a trusted servant of the Crown as well as of two of the leading Marcher lords. In particular it showed Hywel as involved in Edward I's determination to ensure that the royal outposts in Wales were in a state of readiness; it seems quite likely that the king was already preparing for the possibility of conflict with Prince Llywelyn.

It must have been increasingly obvious to the prince that in Hywel ap Meurig he had a dangerous opponent, a man who had contacts within the Welsh community of large swathes of Wales, and who had contacts at the highest levels of royal and Marcher government. There had to be a reckoning, and it came in 1276. In May of that year Hywel was forced by Llywelyn to find sureties in the large sum of one hundred pounds for the release from the prince's prison, and the future loyalty, of Hywel's son John. It seems probable that John had been imprisoned as a hostage to ensure his father's good conduct, though it is also possible that John also was seen as a threat to the prince.[27]

It is the identity of those who stood surety for John's future obedience to Llywelyn that is particularly revealing. They included two of Llywelyn's local officials, the bailiffs of Elfael Is Mynydd and of Gwerthrynion, Ifor ap Gruffudd and Einion ap Madog respectively.[28]

Their future careers and their willingness to act as sureties for Hywel's son would suggest that Llywelyn ap Gruffudd was losing support even amongst his own officers in central Wales. Other sureties included two of the lords of Elfael uwch Mynydd, men who had been conspicuous by their absence from the assembly called by Llywelyn in 1274 to accuse the lord of Powys, Gruffudd ap Gwenwynwyn, of plotting against him.[29] Another surety was Owain ap Meurig of Builth who had already shown himself to have strong connections with the lordship of the Three Castles in Gwent, a territory which was in the possession of Edward I's brother Edmund.[30] It is possible to envisage a growing nexus of leading men of the Middle March who were at least sceptical about the prince's governance and in some cases were downright hostile to it. That nexus of actual and potential opponents of Llywelyn was far-reaching, and it seems clear that Hywel ap Meurig was at the centre of it.

The full extent of Hywel's activities in encouraging opposition to the prince is revealed in the course of the war that broke out between Llywelyn and Edward I in November of 1276. In the course of that conflict, an army some 2,700 strong was formed in the lands of the Middle March. Its purpose was to bring support to other forces that Edward I had in the field. The army was led by Hywel ap Meurig, who was described as the steward of the king, of Humphrey de Bohun, earl of Hereford, and of Roger Mortimer. Of the twenty-seven constables – commanders of one hundred troops – at least twenty were Welsh. They included the prince's former officials Ifor ap Gruffudd and Einion ap Madog, both men with previous connections with Hywel ap Meurig, as well as Llywelyn ap Caradog, Hywel's fellow witness to the Dore charter issued by Meurig ap Gruffudd in 1271. The William ap Hywel who also acted as a constable was almost certainly a son of Hywel ap Meurig.[31]

Hywel had, therefore, played a significant part in destabilising Prince Llywelyn's regime in the Middle March and elsewhere in the 1270s, and had been a vitally important participant in the war which effectively broke Llywelyn's power in large parts of Wales, and confined him to a truncated principality covering only western Gwynedd. Hywel would surely have been justified in looking for rewards for his service, and he was not to be disappointed.

iv. Building a new world

By November of 1277 the war against Llywelyn was over. The Treaty of Aberconwy in that month saw his rule over much of Wales effectively dismantled. Llywelyn retained his title of prince of Wales, but it now had a hollow ring to it. His principality was limited to Gwynedd west of the Conwy and a handful of minor lordships in the Vale of Edeirnion. Lands which Llywelyn had ruled in the rest of Wales were handed back to the Marcher lords whom he had displaced or were given to new lords set up by Edward – men like Roger Mortimer. Edward retained some lands in his own hands and began to build the first of the great castles which were intended to cement his hold on Wales – castles like Flint and Rhuddlan in the north, Aberystwyth in the west and Builth in mid-Wales. At the same time, the political upheavals of the last few years and the chaos of the war had created many problems such as conflicting claims to land, rights to inheritance or claims of injustice in lordly governance throughout much of Wales, and these needed to be settled if many regions were not to descend into violence. As one of those who had been stalwart in securing the triumph of Edward I in the recent war, and who had shown clear signs of administrative and political ability in the years before that war, it was almost inevitable that Hywel ap Meurig should have been called upon to help to secure the new dispensation in Wales.

On 10 January 1278 Edward I, from the Tower of London, issued letters appointing the bishop of Worcester, Master Ralph de Fremingham, Walter de Hopton, Maredudd, archdeacon of Cardigan, Hywel ap Meurig, Goronwy ap Heilyn and Rhys ap Gruffudd as justices in his place, 'to hear and determine all suits and pleas both of lands and of trespasses and wrongs in the Marches and in Wales and to do justice therein according to the laws and customs of the parts in which the lands lie or in which the trespasses and wrongs have been committed'.[32] The persons appointed are of great significance. The bishop of Worcester was probably at the head of the list for form's sake: a prominent ecclesiastic whose nomination would lend a veneer of spiritual rectitude to proceedings, and a man who was evidently not expected to attend the 'business sessions' of the bench of justices. This last point was demonstrated at once, as Ralph de Fremingham and the others were ordered to assemble at Oswestry to begin their hearings, 'without waiting for the presence of G. bishop of Worcester'.[33]

Ralph de Fremingham was a seasoned royal appointee, and a senior judicial figure, being a Justice of Common Pleas, as well as a canon of St Paul's. His career as one of Hywel's colleagues would be short, for he was called to other business on the king's behalf, which involved travel to Rome.[34] Walter de Hopton, on whom the leadership of the Bench of justices then fell, was a Shropshire magnate, and another very experienced judicial figure, a former sheriff of Shropshire and Staffordshire, a baron of the Exchequer and a future justice in Eyre for a large circuit of counties.[35]

The Welsh appointees are equally interesting. Goronwy ap Heilyn acted as a senior official of both Llywelyn ap Gruffudd and Edward I; he was a member of the family of Ednyfed Fychan, the great minister of Llywelyn ab Iorwerth, for he was Ednyfed's nephew. He was destined to lose faith in King Edward and to go over to Llywelyn ap Gruffudd's brother and successor, Dafydd ap Gruffudd. Goronwy acted as Dafydd's *distain*, or chief minister; and he died as a rebel 'against the peace', fighting for the prince.[36] Goronwy ap Heilyn, in other words, was one of the most important political figures in Gwynedd of the thirteenth century. The same may apply to Rhys ap Gruffudd. Here was a grandson of Ednyfed Fychan, and a son of Ednyfed's successor in the office of *distain* in Gwynedd. He would serve both Llywelyn ap Gruffudd and subsequently Edward I. Married to Margaret Lestrange, a member of an important Marcher family, one member of which would command the army that was to kill Llywelyn ap Gruffudd, Rhys ap Gruffudd would rise high in the administration of north Wales under Edward I.[37] Hywel's Welsh companions on the Hopton Bench were thus men of pivotal significance. It says a lot about his standing that his name comes before those of Goronwy ap Heilyn and Rhys ap Gruffudd in the king's commission.

The work of the Hopton bench was arduous; the justices heard hundreds of cases in close to fifty sessions in some three years. And it may be significant that some of the sessions appear to have been held before only Hopton himself and Hywel ap Meurig. One such session took place at Builth in 1278.[38] The fact that Hopton had travelled to Builth is interesting, because it was there that Hywel ap Meurig had developed new responsibilities. Hywel's involvement in the judicial work of the Hopton bench was important enough in establishing Edward I's new order in Wales, but it was far from the only task with which he had been entrusted and which he had seized. For Hywel became, in the years after 1277, a figure of crucial significance in the establishment of royal control of central Wales.

A week before Hywel was appointed to the Hopton commission other letters were issued by the king, which announced that he had committed to Hywel ap Meurig his land and castle of Builth, to hold for a full year for £100, to be paid at the exchequer[39]. Thus, Hywel had become the 'farmer' of the lordship of Builth. As such it is evident that he was responsible for the construction of the great castle that Edward had ordered to be built overlooking the settlement of Llanfair ym Muallt (Builth Wells). The enigmatic remains of that castle remain, though it is the least regarded and least studied of the works that Edward caused to be raised in Wales. In March of 1279, Hywel's custody of the land and castle of Builth was extended, and he was also given responsibility for the custody or rental of a mine there.[40] Hywel was thus put in sole charge of a lordship and castle which were vital to the maintenance of royal power in central Wales.

And beyond Hywel's work with the Hopton bench and at Builth, other judicial duties came his way. In November 1278 Hywel was one of two men, the other being Adam le Botiller, who were commissioned by royal order to hear and determine 'the complaints of certain of the king's men of Abergavenny of trespasses and injuries inflicted on them by Master Henry de Bray the king's steward or his ministers there, and also touching trespasses and injuries done to the king or his bailiffs by certain men of the parts of Abergavenny'.[41] Ultimately Walter de Hopton himself was appointed as an additional justice, and the case was moved before the Hopton bench.[42] In July 1279 Hywel was associated with Roger de Moles, keeper of Llanbadarn and Ceredigion, to hear claims that a descendant of the Lord Rhys, Cynan ap Maredudd ab Owain, had committed trespasses against the abbot and convent of Strata Florida.[43] A few months later Hywel was involved in another case which appears to have run separately from the Hopton bench. This concerned rival claims to lands in west Wales by Hywel and Rhys, sons of Gruffudd (ab Ednyfed Fychan), which he was deputed to hear together with John de Perres.[44] Cases involving members of the ministerial aristocracy of Gwynedd, based on descent from Ednyfed Fychan, husband of Gwenllian daughter of the Lord Rhys, who had claims to rule significant areas of Deheubarth, and were key supporters of Edward I, were sensitive matters, and it is a sign of Hywel's eminence that he was deputed by the king to hear them. And it is clear that Hywel's tasks in the years after 1277 extended to more than a multiplicity of judicial roles and responsibility for the castle and lordship of Builth. Thus, in June of 1280 he was joined by Henry de Bray and by the prominent royal official Bogo de Knovill in the task of delivering to Roger de Mortimer of West Wales land worth fifty pounds per year which had been granted to him by the king.[45]

There can be little doubt that Hywel's importance in central Wales was sometimes expressed in ways which reflected both his official status as a royal official and his social eminence at the centre of a network of regional contacts. An agreement by which Owain ap Meurig pledged lands at Cefn Rhosferig close to Builth castle to Einion ap Madog in exchange for twelve-and-a-half marks of silver in 1278 was witnessed by the lord Hywel ap Meurig, steward of Builth, and was made with his permission (*licencia sua confectum*).[46] Here is one indication of the extent of the control exercised by Hywel in the lordship of Builth. But it is not the only one. It is likely that another of the witnesses, the lord William ap Hywel, parson of Llanwrthwl in the same lordship, is to be identified as Hywel ap Meurig's son.[47] A member of the decanal chapter of Builth, and a future dean of that land, William ap Hywel was one means by which Hywel ap Meurig cemented his influence there. And then there is the matter of the two men most centrally concerned in the pledge of the lands of Cefn Rhosferig: Einion ap Madog and Owain ap Meurig. Both men had in fact been sureties for the future loyalty to Prince Llywelyn of John, son of Hywel ap Meurig, to ensure his release from the prince's prison in 1276.[48] At the time Einion had been Prince Llywelyn's bailiff of Gwerthrynion, but by 1277 he was leading, under Hywel ap Meurig's command, one hundred men of Builth against Llywelyn's forces. Another of the troop leaders from Builth was William ap Hywel, surely the man of that name who was a son of Hywel ap Meurig.[49] And Owain ap Meurig was specifically designated as 'of Builth' in the list of sureties for John ap Hywel in 1276.[50]

In the same year Owain had witnessed and sealed a grant of lands in the lordship of the Three Castles, a grant apparently made in Builth.[51] That grant was also sealed by the dean of Builth, and witnessed by the whole chapter of Builth, amongst whom was presumably William ap Hywel.[52] Thus a socio-political nexus begins to emerge in central Wales at the centre of which was Hywel ap Meurig. And in the background William, Hywel ap Meurig's son was it seems ever-present.

Einion ap Madog and Owain ap Meurig had helped Hywel by becoming sureties for his son in 1276. In 1278 he helped them to reach a mutually advantageous arrangement. There is one more possibility which ought to be considered. The 1278 agreement records that the lands of Cefn Rhosferig had been transferred for a term of 120 years to Einion ap Madog and his children by his wife Lleucu daughter of Hywel, and their heirs.[53] It can only be a matter for speculation, but it seems possible that Lleucu herself may have been a daughter of Hywel ap Meurig.

We can therefore see the official channels through which Hywel ap Meurig built up his position in central Wales in the years after 1276; but we can also glimpse the social nexus within which he worked to consolidate that position. And with his increasing authority and influence came other forms of recognition of his leadership. He had, we know, a seal – in a period when seal usage in central Wales was still developing.[54] And it is clear that at some point, almost certainly in the post-1276 period, he had adopted a coat of arms. His arms appear on St George's Roll of Arms of *c.*1280 under the name Howell ap Meryk, as *Paly d'Or & Az. & i fess Gu. in which are iii mullets Arg.* St George's Roll appears to have been drawn up for the Mortimer family of Wigmore, and very significantly the use of Or and Azure (Gold and Blue) reflects the use of those colours in the arms of the Mortimers.[55] Hywel was thus, it seems, acknowledging the debt which he owed to Mortimer patronage. It is probable that it was at some point in the years after 1276 that his distinguished services to Edward I resulted in his being knighted,[56] a rare distinction for a Welshman. As late as 5 November Hywel, designated as constable of the castle of Builth, and John of Radnor, the king's receiver there, were recorded as being paid £250 owed to the king in order to continue works on the castle.[57]

Throughout the recorded decades of Hywel ap Meurig's career he seems to have been able to move easily from milieux which were predominantly Welsh to association with officials who were overwhelmingly English. Though not the first such 'middle-man', Hywel took to new heights the ability to function in what are increasingly recognised as interlinked rather than simply mutually hostile societies. It is quite clear that although Hywel's principal residence lay just beyond Wales, his administrative appointments had been overwhelmingly focused on the March and *pura Wallia*. Even the able and ambitious sons whom he left had been carefully positioned to continue his family's rise. Those of Hywel's sons who were intended by him to be influential figures of the next generation were clerics, able to move easily in both ecclesiastical and lay environments. In most cases those sons, significantly, were given names that could take both English and Welsh forms: Philip, William/Gwilym, John/Ieuan, the partial exception being Rees.[58] Their names facilitated progress in both cultural environments, and especially in the March.

It was thus that late in 1281, before the final clash with Llywelyn ap Gruffudd, Hywel ap Meurig died, full of honours.[59] The executors of his will were two of his sons, the ubiquitous William, and the highly talented Philip, who rendered his father's final account for Builth.[60]

Intermezzo:
The Sons of Hywel ap Meurig

Hywel ap Meurig's wife, together with his sons and daughters, are recorded in the Welsh chronicle as having been captured with him in 1262. At that point she is unnamed, but a wife who had survived Hywel for several years is recorded in 1297 as holding lands in Herefordshire worth over £20 per year. The widow of 1297 was named as Matilda.[61] Her name strongly suggests that she was English. Like so many of his descendants it seems that Hywel had married into an English family, and it is interesting that from an early period in the family's history sons were given names which were intelligible in an English context while 'converting' easily into names known in Welsh environments.[62] One of his sons, John/? Ieuan ap Hywel, has been noticed as a prisoner of Prince Llywelyn in 1276. His freedom was then being negotiated, and sureties for £100 were assembled by Hywel to guarantee John's future loyalty to the prince. It is not known whether John survived his imprisonment for long, and it is ominous that there are no further clear references to him.

There were clearly other sons, and in some cases their careers can be traced. One such was William ap Hywel, who appears to have had strong connections with Builth. He appears first in a military context, operating under Hywel's command in 1277 and acting as a mounted constable, leading a body of one hundred foot-soldiers from Builth against Prince Llywelyn.[63] In 1278 he was recorded as parson of Llanwrthwl in Builth lordship.[64] By 1281 he was an executor of Hywel's will, together with his brother Philip ap Hywel. In the next year he was appointed, along with one Stephen de Knylle, to store the castle of Builth with provisions, and the two men received safe conducts to enable them to go about that task.[65] At that point William was described as a chaplain, confirming that he had entered the ranks of the clergy. This was certainly the case by the early 1290s, for in 1293 he was recorded as one of the two chief taxators of the land of Builth.[66]

In that record he was described as the dean of Builth; his fellow chief taxator, Einion ap Madog, was almost certainly the man of that name who had been a close friend of Hywel ap Meurig, and may have been married to one of Hywel's daughters, Lleucu.[67] It is possible that the office of dean, the senior clerical post within the lordship of Builth with its half-dozen churches, was the summit of William's achievements in terms of official appointments, for he cannot be identified with confidence in any further records. But he was reputed in genealogical sources to have been the father of Philip de Clanvowe, who would be prominent in the next generation of the family.[68]

The absence of William ap Hywel from records after the early 1290s is matched by a somewhat similar absence of references for long periods to two other brothers, Philip and Rees. Philip, as we have seen, was co-executor with William of his father's will in 1281. But after this the records for Philip are largely silent for around a decade. The single exception is a telling one. Both William and Philip appear as witnesses to a charter of Edmund Mortimer of Wigmore in 1285, in which he grants lands formerly held by Gruffudd ab Owain in Elfael Uwch Mynydd to one of his retainers, Walter Hakelutel.[69] The witness list is headed by kinsfolk of Edmund, and by several knights of the Mortimer affinity. Philip and William – in that order, suggesting Philip's seniority, are the first of several Welsh witnesses. This episode suggests that Philip and William were in the service of Mortimer of Wigmore, as their father had been, and that like him they were significant figures in the upper ranks of Marcher society.

In the case of Rees, apart from his ordination as a sub-deacon in 1287 record sources do not provide any information until the early fourteenth century.[70] It is possible that Rees was younger than William and Philip. If we assume that his father was born in the 1220s and was thus well into his manhood when he appears as a royal arbitrator in the late 1250s, Hywel ap Meurig may well have been producing children from about 1250 onwards. His older sons may have been born in that period: to judge from the 1262 entries in the Welsh chronicles it seems that he had several children by that date. But it is reasonable to suppose that he would have been quite capable of fathering children for years after that, so we may have to envisage children of very different ages. Philip, for example, like his brother William, was clearly of age by 1281; he was regarded as his father's heir, so he may have been the oldest son to have survived to that date. But Rees first becomes visible, fleetingly, in 1287 and is recorded as undertaking official duties only early in the next century. He may thus have been some years younger than Philip.

We may not be far wrong in assuming that some of Hywel's sons died before they could make much of a mark on political life (John for example?) or were of relatively modest attainments. But it is clear that Philip and Rees, and to a lesser degree William, rose to be very significant administrative and political figures. They were amongst the most influential Welshmen of their day. Rees was frequently designated as *Magister*, suggesting that he had spent long years in the developing university system studying and succeeding in both the *trivium*, the programme of instruction in grammar, logic and rhetoric, and the *quadrivium*, which embraced the study of arithmetic, geometry, music and astronomy. The minimum length of study for the degree of Magister was six years – and studies in one of the higher faculties, of Theology, Medicine or Law, would take many more years. Rees ap Hywel was thus very highly educated, and like Philip appears to have become a senior figure in the diocese of St Davids. He was recorded as a prebendary in 1328,[71] and Philip as archdeacon of Brecon in the same year.[72] William ap Hywel was also ordained and rose to be the dean of Builth. It seems that Hywel had decided that an ecclesiastical career was the surest route to advancement for his sons. He may also have hoped that entry into the church would prove a relatively safe route to wealth and influence. If so, he had no idea of the perilous paths that Philip and Rees would sometimes tread.

Notes

1   See R. W. Eyton, *Antiquities of Shropshire*, IV (London, 1857), pp. 247–9.
2   Smith, 'The Middle March', p. 91, no. 9.
3   See *Calendar of Liberate Rolls, 1251–60*, p. 480*; *Calendar of Patent Rolls, 1258–66*, pp. 45*, 65*; *Close Rolls 1259–61*, pp. 89, 310; *Close Rolls, 1261–64*, p. 136. See also payments made to the same group of envoys, including 'Eweyn f. Meurik, recorded in the 1259 Pipe Roll: Richard Cassidy, *The Great Roll of the Pipe for the 43rd Year of the Reign of King Henry III*

Michaelmas 1259, p. 201, available at *http://cmjk.com/1259/1259_pipe_ roll_files/1259_transcript.pdf* (accessed 23 August 2020).

4 Instances are marked with * in the list in the previous note; one of the other negotiators is given as Howen ap Madog and is to be identified as Hywel ap Madog, one of the brothers of Gruffudd ap Madog of northern Powys. This suggests a confusion on the part of the chancery clerk(s) between Owen and Hywel. On the other hand, it is just possible, though unlikely, that we are dealing with a man who was named Owain ap Meurig, and who was to be close to Hywel ap Meurig in the 1270s: on this man, see pp. 19, 23–4.

5 *Close Rolls, 1259–61*, p. 120.

6 For Hywel ap Madog, see David Stephenson, *Medieval Powys: Kingdom, Principality and Lordships, 1132–1293* (Woodbridge: Boydell Press, 2016), pp. 203, 283; for Ednyfed Fychan, see *idem*, *Political Power in Medieval Gwynedd: Governance and the Welsh Princes* (Cardiff: University of Wales Press, 2014), pp. 207–9.

7 Ibid., pp. 219–20.

8 Ibid., pp. 213–14, 220.

9 *Calendar of Patent Rolls, 1258–66*, p. 248.

10 The most fundamental account remains that of J. R. Maddicott, *Simon de Montfort* (Cambridge: Cambridge University Press, 1994), pp. 279–345.

11 The de Bohuns had acquired Brecon lordship by the marriage of Eleanor de Braose (one of the heiresses of William de Braose who died in 1230) with Sir Humphrey de Bohun, who predeceased his father in 1265. Sir Humphrey's son, however, eventually succeeded to the earldom of Hereford, after the death of his grandfather in 1275.

12 London, The National Archives, E 101/3/11. See also p. 19.

13 See p. 7 and note 11.

14 See, for example, Alan Brooks and Nikolaus Pevsner, *The Buildings of England: Herefordshire* (London: Yale University Press, 2012), pp. 406–7.

15 See Lawrence Banks, 'Three houses on one estate', *Transactions of the Radnorshire Society*, 72 (2012), 121–38, at p. 122.

16 The charter is edited by David Stephenson, 'Conquerors, courtiers and careerists: the struggle for supremacy in Brycheiniog, 1093–1282', *Brycheiniog*, XLIV (2013), 27–51, at pp. 50–1.

17 For a discussion of the rapidity of the erosion of Prince Llywelyn's principality as granted to him in 1267, see David Stephenson, 'A treaty too far? The impact of the treaty of Montgomery on Llywelyn ap Gruffudd's principality of Wales', *Montgomeryshire Collections*, 106 (2018), 19–32.

18 Stephenson, 'Conquerors, courtiers and careerists', p. 43.

19 Ibid.

20 Ibid.

21 Walter ap Rhys's given name was a typical Clifford name; Gruffudd ap Cliffo may well have been an illegitimate son of one of the Cliffords.

22 See J. G. Edwards (ed.), *Littere Wallie* (Cardiff: University of Wales Press, 1940), pp. 24–6, 30.

23 J. G. Edwards (ed.), *Calendar of Ancient Correspondence concerning Wales* (Cardiff: University of Wales Press, 1935), p. 49.

24 See, for example, L. Alcock, D. J. C. King, W. G. Putnam, C. J. Spurgeon, 'Excavations at Castell Bryn Amlwg', *Montgomeryshire Collections*, 60 (1967–8), 8–27, especially the following comment by Spurgeon, at p. 25: 'It is tempting to wonder whether the flanking towers and the first period of the gatehouse at Bryn Amlwg represent the work of Llywelyn during his occupation of Temseter (*c.*1267–76). They might even represent the castle which Hywel ap Meurig heard was projected in about 1274.'

25 *Calendar of Close Rolls, 1279–86*, p. 260.

26 *Calendar of Patent Rolls, 1272–81*, p. 119.

27 Edwards (ed.), *Littere Wallie*, pp. 32–3, 41–2, 44.

28 Ibid., pp. 41–2.

29 Ibid., pp. 98–9, 108–10. Of the two lords of Elfael is Mynydd, Iorwerth ab Owain and Madog ab Owain, the latter subsequently refused to act as a surety and had to be replaced.

30 Ibid., pp. 41–2; for his connection with the lordship of Three Castles, see David Stephenson, 'New light on a dark deed: the death of Llywelyn ap Gruffudd, prince of Wales', *Archaeologia Cambrensis*, 166 (2017), 243–52, passim. Even the abbot of Cwmhir was pressed into standing surety for John ap Hywel ap Meurig's future loyalty in the substantial sum of forty pounds, an act which is explicitly recorded as being 'at the instance of the noble man Hywel ap Meurig': Edwards (ed.), *Littere Wallie*, pp. 32–3.

31 For William ap Hywel, see pp. 19, 23–4, 26–7.

32 J. Conway Davies (ed.), *The Welsh Assize Roll 1277–84* (Cardiff: University of Wales Press, 1940), p. 86.

33 *Calendar of Various Chancery Rolls (Welsh Rolls)*, p. 163.

34 *Welsh Assize Roll*, pp. 98–9.

35 Ibid., pp. 100–4.

36 Stephenson, *Political Power*, pp. 213–14.

37 Ibid., p. 218.

38 *Welsh Assize Roll*, p. 243.

39 *Calendar of Various Chancery Rolls (Welsh Rolls)*, p. 178.

40 Ibid.; *Calendar of Patent Rolls, 1272–81*, p. 304.

41 *Calendar of Patent Rolls, 1272–81*, p. 294.

42 Ibid., p. 339.

43 *Calendar of Various Chancery Rolls (Welsh Rolls)*, p. 179.

[44] Ibid., pp. 179–80, where the justices are referred to as Hywel ap Maredudd and John de Perres; the first name is almost certainly an error for Hywel ap Meurig. The same mistake was made with respect to Hywel ap Meurig's appointment to the Hopton Commission in January 1278: ibid., p. 163.

[45] Ibid., pp. 185–6.

[46] *Welsh Assize Roll*, p. 299.

[47] Ibid.

[48] *Littere Wallie*, pp. 41–2.

[49] London, The National Archives, E 101/3/11. The names of the constables and the payments are all recorded on a membrane pencil-marked '3'.

[50] *Littere Wallie*, pp. 41–2.

[51] David Stephenson, 'Empires in Wales: from Gruffudd ap Llywelyn to Llywelyn ap Gruffudd', *Welsh History Review*, 28/1 (2016), 26–54, at 49–53.

[52] He is recorded as parson of Llanwrthwl (in the lordship/deanery of Builth) only two years later: *Welsh Assize Roll*, p. 299.

[53] Ibid.

[54] For a discussion of developing seal-usage, see the review article by David Stephenson, 'Seals in medieval Wales', *Archaeologia Cambrensis*, 166 (2017), 323–31.

[55] On St George's Roll, see N. Denholm-Young, *History and Heraldry 1254–1310* (Oxford: The Clarendon Press, 1965), especially pp. 90–5. See also Michael Powell Siddons, *The Development of Welsh Heraldry* II (Aberystwyth: National Library of Wales, 1993), p. 260, though the notes to this entry are not entirely reliable.

[56] *Welsh Assize Roll*, p. 117.

[57] *Calendar of Close Rolls, 1279–88*, p. 284.

[58] It is, however, perhaps significant that his name is given in the 'Frenchified' form of Reys fitzHowell in the record of his ordination as a sub-deacon in 1287: see note 70 below.

[59] We can be sure that Hywel died late in 1281. On 28 November of that year an order was issued to the auditors of the account of Hywel ap Meurig, the king's late bailiff of Builth to allow to the executors of Hywel's will twenty marks that the king granted him for his office for Michaelmas term last.

[60] *BBCS*, 28 (1978–80), 268; Griffiths, *Principality of Wales*, p. 97; WG: 801. Hywel's final account for the castle and land of Builth is given in the Pipe Roll for 1282 (TNA 372/126, 10 Edward I) under the Herefordshire accounts, with a note that his son and heir Philip had rendered the account for Hywel because of the latter's death.

[61] A list of Herefordshire military summonses of those who held property worth £20 per annum in 1297 includes *Matild(a) que fuit uxor Howeli ap Meurik*; see *Parliamentary Writs and Writs of Military Summons*, p. 286.

[62] See the genealogical chart above, p. xv, for several examples of Philip, and of John, as well as William/Gwilym.

[63] London, The National Archives, E 101/3/11.

[64] *Welsh Assize Roll*, p. 299.

[65] *Calendar of Patent Rolls, 1281–92*, p. 15.

[66] Francis Jones (ed.), 'The subsidy of 1292', *Bulletin of the Board of Celtic Studies*, 13 (1950), p. 221.

[67] See p. 24.

[68] Bartrum, *Welsh Genealogies*, IV, Rhys ap Tewdwr 26.

[69] *Calendar of Charter Rolls, 1257–1300*, p. 304. Gruffudd ab Owain had been one of the Welsh lords of Elfael Uwch Mynydd: see Huw Pryce (ed.), *The Acts of Welsh Rulers 1120–1283* (Cardiff: University of Wales Press, 2005), no. 106. For Philip's further relations with Walter Hakelutel, see p. 37 below.

[70] William W. Capes (ed.), *Registrum Ricardi de Swinfield* (London: Canterbury and York Society, 1909), p. 548.

[71] B. Jones (ed.), *Fasti Ecclesiae Anglicanae 1300–1541: Volume 11, the Welsh Dioceses (Bangor, Llandaff, St Asaph, St Davids)* (London: Institute of Historical Research, 1965), p. 80.

[72] Ibid., p. 61.

3

Philip ap Hywel: Administrative Eminence and Political Peril

i. Consolidating a career

After Philip ap Hywel's appearance as one of the executors of his father's will, and a similar appearance as accounting for his father's tenure of the post of steward of Builth, he does not appear in the extant records for nearly a decade. We are not to assume that he was idle in that period, however, for when he reappears it is in a very senior position. In 1290 Philip sealed an agreement whereby he undertook the custody of Dryslwyn castle and lands of the rebel Rhys ap Maredudd, for an entire year in exchange for a fee of £200 from the king.[1] He had therefore already emerged as a prominent royal official. In the records of the officials and jurors involved in the assessment and collection of the lay subsidy of 1292, a tax levied by Edward I throughout Wales, Philip ap Hywel appears as the steward of Humphrey de Bohun, earl of Hereford and lord of Brecon, in both the lordship of Brecon and that of Hay and Huntingdon.[2] Philip occurs again as the earl's steward in Brecon some five years later, in very interesting circumstances.

In 1297 Edward I was clearly trying to undermine the power of the earl of Hereford in the Marches. It would seem that the king sent one of his closest Welsh servants and allies, Morgan ap Maredudd, into the region of the lordship of Brecon to stir up resentment against, and opposition to, the earl.[3] It was not the first time that we may suspect that Morgan ap Maredudd had acted as an agent provocateur. In 1283 he had appeared as a prominent figure in the entourage of Prince Dafydd ap Gruffudd in the final stages of the prince's war with

Edward I; Dafydd was of course executed later that year; his sons suffered close imprisonment; yet nothing adverse seems to have happened to Morgan ap Maredudd.[4] In 1294–5 Morgan had led a rebellion in Glamorgan but had successfully claimed that it was directed against Gilbert de Clare, earl of Gloucester and lord of Glamorgan, rather than against the king.[5] In 1295 Morgan appears to have been closely involved in a conspiracy with the French king and with the rebel lord Thomas Turberville. There was documentary evidence of Morgan's involvement, but once again he survived, and even prospered.[6] The evidence of the king's continued confidence in Morgan ap Maredudd is to be found in the 1297 episode relating to the lordship of Brecon.

That Morgan had been entrusted by the king with a very sensitive mission is indicated by a record that he had been sent into Wales in the late summer of 1297 'on certain secret business of the king, by the special order of the king himself'.[7] It would appear that his task was to provoke a revolt against the earl of Hereford's governance, which would be the pretext for Edward I's seizure into his own hand of the lordship of Brecon. But Morgan had to report to the king that before his coming the earl of Hereford had sent John le Rose to Philip ap Hywel, the earl's steward of Brecon to organise provisions for the earl's castles and to inform the men of the country that the earl was against the king's peace.

> Next Philip ap Hywel and John le Rose had called all the men of [the lordship of] Brecon before them, and had granted to them, in the earl's name, and by a good charter, all the laws and usages that they had ever had in the times of his ancestors, and had pardoned them many things … And on the same day as he came to Morgannwg, Morgan sent certain men into Brycheiniog, and the next day he spoke to those of that land whom he knew best, and he asked if there was no-one who would [reject the grants] which the earl had made to them, and they replied that they were all at one with their lord …

At this point Morgan, clearly aware that he had been out-manoeuvred, asked that he might know the king's will in the matter.[8]

So, Philip ap Hywel had been instrumental in heading off Morgan ap Maredudd's attempted subversion of the earl of Hereford's control of Brecon lordship, and as such had undoubtedly enhanced his standing in the earl's eyes. But that was by no means the sum of Philip's endeavours in 1297 for it was in early June of the same year that he had been present in an elite group of witnesses, including the earl of Arundel, the abbots of Wigmore and Cwmhir, two knights and a member of the influential de Lingayne family, when Edmund Mortimer had responded to the complaints against him by the men of Maelienydd.[9] He had conceded to them, in exchange for a payment of five hundred pounds, an extensive list of traditional rights and the redress of grievances against unjust impositions with which he had burdened them. It may be no coincidence that the common factor in the charters issued by both Edmund Mortimer in Maelienydd and Humphrey de Bohun in Brycheiniog within a few weeks in the summer of 1297 was the man who acted as steward to them both, Philip ap Hywel.

This remarkable double stewardship did not exhaust Philip's energies, for after the grant of the Maelienydd charters and before the rapid and successful moves to counter Morgan ap Maredudd's probing of the loyalties of the men of Brecon lordship, Philip ap Hywel had demonstrated his usefulness to the king himself. On 13 July a royal writ announced that troops levied in West Wales and in the March for service with the king overseas were to muster at Hereford where they would be put under the direction of the sheriff of Herefordshire and Philip ap Hywel.[10] It almost certainly took more than a little political finesse to support King Edward's military plans on the one hand, while thwarting the same monarch's attempts to destabilise the earl of Hereford's control of Brecon on the other.

In the next year, 1298, Philip appears in circumstances which suggest that he was consolidating another facet of his career. We know that he was his father's principal heir, and that he lived at Hergest, the house in the lordship of Huntingdon which it seems that Hywel ap Meurig had built. In the course of a visitation by bishop Swinfield of Kington, the parish in which Hergest lay, Philip entertained the bishop, for Swinfield's household roll contains the information that the bishop 'was at dinner with the lord Philip ap Hywel at Hergest'.[11] In the closing years of the century Philip ap Hywel was keeping company with some very influential people and was clearly establishing his usefulness with many of them. It comes therefore as no surprise when in 1299 we find that Philip had been commissioned by royal order to hold the castle of Builth for five years at a rent of £113 6s. 8d per year.[12] At a relatively early stage of his career he was as prominent in the affairs of the March as his father had been at the time of his death.

ii. From administration to high politics

For well over a decade Philip ap Hywel resembled the typical diligent clerical servant of the English royal government. On occasion he was described as the king's clerk, and the range of duties which he undertook for Edward I and Edward II was considerable. He maintained his possession of Builth castle for many years, his commission being renewed for five years in 1304 and for a further two years in 1309.[13]

He was associated more than once with Walter de Pederton, who served for several periods as Justiciar and deputy justiciar in west Wales. In 1301 the two of them, together with Philip's brother Rees, were appointed to pay troops raised in west Wales their wages until they reached Carlisle en route to Scotland.[14] In 1307 Philip, still holding the castle of Builth, received a royal order to repair the houses and walls, the works to be viewed by Walter de Pederton.[15] Walter and Philip were also ordered to cause the collectors of a tax of one twentieth of moveables which had been granted to Edward I to come before them to account, and to make arrangements to pay arrears.[16] In July of 1308 Philip was associated with Walter de Pederton once more, and, ironically, with his adversary in Brecon in 1297, Morgan ap Maredudd, to levy 600 troops in South Wales and Cardigan.[17] These men were to be led to Carlisle by Morgan and by Walter de Hakelut. It would appear that Morgan was the adventurer, and employed as such, whereas Philip was the administrator.

A duty of a very different type fell to Philip in October of 1308. This time he was associated with one John Poleyne. They were required by the king to deliver to John son of Reginald the issues, castles and towns of Blaenllyfni and Bwlchydinas, the town and manor of Talgarth as well as the manor of Caldecot in Gwent, which had been granted by John son of Reginald to the king, and then granted back to John for his lifetime.[18] John had evidently not lived long to enjoy his lifetime grant, for he was dead within eighteen months. In February of 1310 John's lands were granted to Roger Mortimer of Chirk at the rent fixed by a survey held in the Exchequer. The person required to deliver the lands to Mortimer was Philip ap Hywel, a fact which suggests that Philip had been custodian of those lands after John's death.[19] There appears to have been an exception to the grant of John son of Reginald's lands to Mortimer, that being the manor of Caldecot. This was granted to John de Sapy, recorded as king's yeoman, in March 1310. Again, it was Philip ap Hywel who received the royal order to deliver the manor to Sapy.[20] A further part of John fitz Reginald's lands which did not find its way into Mortimer's hands was the manor of Talgarth, and it is possible that Philip was in some way involved in this matter. For as we shall see, Talgarth fell by agreement to Philip's brother, Rees ap Hywel.[21]

But while it is clear that Philip ap Hywel was frequently active in royal service, it is just as evident that he had retained his links with the Mortimers. There are indeed hints that Philip was very close to Roger Mortimer of Wigmore, the successor to Edmund for whom he had acted as steward. It is probable that Philip was closely involved in the financial affairs of the lord of Wigmore, as evidenced in a record of March 1308 of a debt of 1,000 marks owed to Philip de Kyme by Roger Mortimer of Wigmore, Margaret late wife of Edmund Mortimer, Joan late the wife of John Wake and Philip ap Hywel.[22] It would seem that Philip may have been in a position to lend large sums to the Mortimer family, a suspicion strengthened by a record of February 1310, which reveals that Roger Mortimer, this time Mortimer of Chirk, together with Walter Hakelutel, Thomas de Roshale, Hugh de Croft and Philip ap Hywel owed Edmund Hakelutel £720.[23] This is followed by a further record that Roger Mortimer of Chirk owes Walter, Thomas, Hugh and Philip £720.[24] It seems likely that the four men named with Mortimer had agreed to guarantee his repayment of a debt to Edmund Hakelutel.

Another transaction which took place in February of 1310 involved a royal grant to Roger Mortimer of Wigmore of the castle of Builth, at the same rent which Philip ap Hywel, late constable, used to pay.[25] So it is clear that Philip's tenure of Builth castle had been abruptly terminated before the due date of his grant. It is perhaps possible that the grant to Mortimer was arranged to help him find surety for his debt to Philip de Kyme, for the arrangement was of brief duration: by

December 1310 Mortimer had given up the keeping of Builth castle, and was instructed to deliver it once more to Philip ap Hywel, who was to hold it during the king's pleasure.[26] This time Philip's control of Builth lasted until early in 1314, when he was instructed to hand it over to John Charlton, the lord of Powys.[27] Charlton had been struggling to maintain his hold on the great barony of Powys against a determined attempt by his wife's uncle, Gruffudd Fychan, to take the lands and castle from him. In the course of the conflict, which assumed the proportions of a private war in mid-Wales, the castle of La Pole (today's Powis) had been seriously damaged by Gruffudd Fychan's forces.[28] To rebuild the castle and to strengthen it Charlton needed money, and it seems that as a prominent courtier – Edward II's chamberlain – he had prevailed on the king to grant him Builth.[29]

It was perhaps predictable that Charlton's grasping and oppressive administration would lead to an outcry. By May of 1315 the king was forced to launch an enquiry into the excesses of the keeper of the castle and his ministers. The enquiry was entrusted in June to William Martyn and William Bagot, but Bagot was replaced in December by Philip ap Hywel.[30] It is possible that Philip had not been available to undertake the enquiry in a land which he knew well as he had been assigned another task in April of 1315: this was to work with William le Butler, lord of Wem, to investigate complaints by the burgesses of Montgomery that the men of the nearby town of Chirbury had instituted a market, 'to the injury of the market and fairs of Montgomery'.[31]

The enquiries at Montgomery and Builth called for firmness and tact as well as administrative ability, but they were insignificant in comparison with the much greater task with which Philip was entrusted in the autumn of 1315. In the spring of that year, following his great victory over Edward II's forces at Bannockburn, Robert the Bruce had decided to broaden the war by sending his brother Edward to open a new front in Ireland, where he landed in May with a Scottish army. Bruce made significant progress in the following months, and numerous Irish lords began to recognise him as the king of Ireland. In England, the government began to fear that Bruce would be able to construct a 'Celtic alliance'.[32] As a consequence Edward II began to prepare for Scottish landings in Wales. The king's meetings with

Welsh magnates such as Sir Gruffudd Llwyd and Morgan ap Maredudd are relatively well known. Much less familiar, but just as important, is his reliance on certain other Welsh leaders. This is the background to an order addressed to the chamberlain of Caernarfon, one of the most powerful ministers in the principality of North Wales. He was instructed:

> to expend such money about the defense and custody of the parts of Wales as shall be directed by Master John Walwayn, escheator this side of Trent, Philip ap Hywel and Master Rees ap Hywel whom the king is sending thither to ordain, together with John de Grey, Justice of North Wales for the defense of Wales against the threatened invasion of the Scots rebels who lately attacked Ireland, and to aid the said Justice and John, Philip and Rees.[33]

A separate order was sent to the chamberlain of Carmarthen, in charge of the finances of the southern Principality, with William Martyn Justice of south Wales – and Philip's former colleague in the Builth enquiry – replacing John de Grey. In other words, Philip and his brother Rees, along with John Walwayn and the relevant Justiciars, were being made directly responsible for the material organisation of Wales in the face of the threat from the Bruces.[34] In the northern principality the bishops, abbots and other ecclesiastical magnates received letters ordering them to give credence to John de Grey and to John and Philip in what they should inform them on the king's behalf and to execute what they should direct. It is clear that the king had given full powers to organise the principality lands and resources to his representatives, and that Philip and Rees were acting at the highest levels of politics in Wales.

The crisis caused by Bruce's invasion of Ireland passed without a similar expedition into Wales, and Philip and William Martyn were able to return to other duties. One such was to permit a meeting between the men of the lands of Builth and the ministers against whom they had complained in order to settle the matter by agreement.[35] By 1315/16, then, Philip had emerged as one of the stalwarts of royal administration in Wales. But that situation was to change dramatically in the years to come and was to endanger all that Philip had achieved.

iii. In danger: the perils of politics

Philip was still an important member of the Mortimer affinity in 1316, as is demonstrated by his appointment, together with John de Hothum, to act as grantees of all of the lands in Wales and several English counties which belonged to Roger Mortimer of Wigmore. Philip and Hothum were then to re-grant them to Mortimer on terms which enabled the lord of Wigmore to specify more precisely the descent of the lands after his death.[36] This was a common enough procedure, but it required the participation, as initial grantees, of persons in whom the grantor had complete confidence.

After 1316, however, the records once more become silent as to Philip's activities. These were troubled times, and it is easy to explain Philip's absence from official government records. A large portion of the baronage of Edward II's realm, including many of the Marcher lords, grew increasingly exasperated at the king's dependence on his favourites, the Despensers. In 1321 a war broke out in the March, particularly in Glamorgan, which had been granted to Hugh Despenser the Younger. Hugh the Younger was particularly close to the king, who was described by one chronicler as loving him dearly with all his heart and mind. His misrule in Glamorgan, which included the murder of the rebel leader Llywelyn Bren, for whom both Roger Mortimer of Wigmore and Humphrey de Bohun had interceded with the king, prompted the Marchers, led by Thomas, earl of Lancaster, to rise against him.[37] By July the rebel forces had even occupied London, and the king was forced to exile the Despensers in order to stave off the threat of his own deposition. By August of 1321 Edward began the process of pardoning the chief rebels, including Lancaster, Humphrey de Bohun, and the Mortimers, and then their leading followers. Amongst those pardoned at the behest of Humphrey de Bohun, earl of Hereford was Philip ap Hywel.[38]

It seems probable that Philip, as a known associate of the Mortimers and of the earl of Hereford, had moved away from royal service as the king's alienation of the Marchers had increased. By 1321 it is evident that Philip had supported the Marchers in their rebellion. He, like many others, was pardoned while the Marcher lords held the initiative. But the crisis was far from over. King Edward began plotting his revenge on the Marcher lords, particularly Thomas of Lancaster, the Mortimers and Humphrey de Bohun. Late in 1321 war broke out again, and this time Edward was able to seize the initiative. First the Mortimers surrendered, and then on 16 March 1322 the royal forces met with the remnant of the opposition forces at Boroughbridge, north-west of York. Humphrey de Bohun was killed, and Thomas of Lancaster captured and executed. The Despensers had already been pardoned and recalled.[39] Even before Boroughbridge, as soon as it was clear that the king's forces were in the ascendant, the reprisals against supporters of baronial leaders like the Mortimers, de Bohun and Lancaster had begun. On 16 February orders were issued for the arrest of some of those suspected of treasonable intentions, and they included Philip ap Hywel and his brother Rees, along with others of Hywel ap Meurig's descendants.[40]

Boroughbridge marked the quickening of the campaign by Edward to destroy whatever survived of the opposition to his rule. Courts dispensed summary justice, and many of those who had been associated with the leaders of the baronial party were executed. Others were imprisoned, including the Mortimers, Roger Mortimer of Wigmore and his uncle Roger Mortimer of Chirk, whose surrender saved their lives. But both were consigned to the Tower of London. It is in this context that we hear once again of Philip ap Hywel. In May of 1322 a royal order was dispatched to Master John Walwayn – Philip's colleague in arranging the defence of Wales in 1315 – and his associate Robert de Morby, both trusted officers of the king. They were ordered to release several captives from the Middle March. Some bore the names of distinguished Marcher families: such were Richard de Baskerville, Philip and John Havard, Philip and John Parpoint, and Miles Pychard – all members of the de Bohun affinity, with lands and family connections in the de Bohun lordship of Brecon. Several of those now released were amongst those whose arrest had been ordered in February.[41] And second on the list of those to be released comes the name of Philip ap Hywel.[42] Though released, the former prisoners were not by any means in the clear. The instructions given to John Walwayn and Robert de Morby were to ensure that the prisoners were to provide mainpernors (effectively guarantors) to have them before the king at his order to answer to him. Philip may have persuaded the royal authorities that he had not played an active part in the movement in which Humphrey de Bohun and the Mortimers had been so prominent, for in July 1322 a royal officer, Roger Carles, was ordered to restore to Philip ap Hywel his lands and goods, the custody whereof was delivered to Roger by the sheriff of Herefordshire, by whom they had been taken into the king's hands because it was said that Philip adhered to Humphrey de Bohun, and that he wore Humphrey's robes for a long time.[43] Here we have valuable evidence that Philip had continued his association with the earl of Hereford as well as that with the Mortimers. His brother Rees was also deeply and dangerously implicated in the movement against the king, as we shall see. In those circumstances Philip was very lucky to escape further punishment. He had presumably managed to convince the king or his advisers that he posed no threat.

There is evidence that he was several times persuaded to stand surety for some of those under suspicion of being opponents of the king, and his situation cannot have been made easier when his former lord, Roger Mortimer of Wigmore, succeeded in escaping from the Tower of London in August of 1323.[44] Once clear of the Tower, Roger made his way to France, from where he could begin to plot the downfall of Edward II. A known associate of Mortimer's such as Philip must have known that he was in grave danger of being a victim of the government's resolve that potential followers of Mortimer should not be allowed freedom to act.

iv. Survival and recovery

With the triumph of Edward II over his baronial enemies we enter once again a period in which references to Philip's activities are very few in official records. One document which does not emanate from government records does, however, shed a most interesting light on Philip's life after 1322. In a charter dated at Pool Castle on 19 April 1324 John Charlton, lord of Powys, confirmed and extended lands which had originally been granted to the burgesses of Welshpool by his predecessor, Owain ap Gruffudd ap Gwenwynwyn, for the pasturing of their beasts. Among the witnesses to this charter, attesting in second place after Sir John Hinckley, is Lord Philip ap Hywel, canon of St Davids.[45]

It should be noted at once that Philip had no official business as a canon of St Davids at Pool Castle, as the castle and its lands lay within the diocese of St Asaph. It is probable that his presence at Pool had a quite different purpose. John Charlton had been politically close to Roger Mortimer of Wigmore, whose daughter Maud was married to Charlton's son John. He had joined in the revolt of the Marcher lords against the king in 1321, and all his lands were confiscated by the king in January 1322 at about the time of the surrender of the Mortimers to Edward.[46] But Charlton, a former chamberlain of the king and the recipient of many grants from him, apparently succeeded in returning to royal favour. Within a week of the king's victory over Thomas of Lancaster and Humphrey de Bohun in March 1322, Charlton was apparently once more in royal service, leading troops for the king in Scotland.[47]

John Charlton of Powys thus appears as a former member of the baronial opposition to Edward, who had weighed up the military situation after the Mortimers were taken into custody and decided that safety lay in a return to his former loyalty to Edward, at least on the surface. It is almost certain that Charlton's submission to the king was made simply to save his skin and that his real sympathies still lay with Roger Mortimer of Wigmore. As soon as Mortimer had returned to England in 1326, this time in the company of Edward's estranged wife Isabella, by then Mortimer's lover, John Charlton began hunting down the doomed king's favourites. These included the earl of Arundel, who was captured at Shrewsbury by Charlton, and sent to Hereford for execution.[48]

The lord of Powys thus appears to have been an ideal protector for Philip ap Hywel. He was a secret adherent of Philip's former lord, and yet he had convinced the king of his loyalty, so that royal intervention in his lordship was unlikely. Philip's appearance at Pool castle thus gives us a valuable clue to how he managed to survive through the years of the Despensers' ascendancy from 1322 to 1326. It is likely that John Charlton was able to offer him a safe haven when it was needed. More than that, it is hard to resist the suspicion that Philip ap Hywel may have been acting as a Mortimer agent in talks with John Charlton.

Roger Mortimer had escaped to France in August 1323, and by early 1324 there were many rumours of Mortimer plots. It is entirely possible that Philip's presence in Pool Castle was connected with just such a Mortimer enterprise. It may not be without significance that Sir John Hinckley, the Staffordshire knight whose name precedes that of Philip ap Hywel in the 1324 charter, apparently made a timely submission to Edward II at about the same time as the surrender of the Mortimers in early 1322.[49]

It is also significant that the 1324 charter places emphasis on Philip's position as a canon of St Davids. A rise to a position of some eminence in the diocese was another way of establishing a position of safety from the increasing tyranny of the Despensers. Indeed, as far as the scanty evidence can be trusted, Philip's last years appear to have been much occupied with ecclesiastical business and the acquisition of positions of importance within the church. In 1328 he appears as the archdeacon of Brecon within the diocese of St Davids.[50] This post gave him ecclesiastical authority throughout the Middle March, the region most central to the political affairs of his family.

And perhaps as significant, Philip appears to have advanced his position within the diocese of Hereford, in the region adjacent to the March. Within that diocese he had for many years been a portioner (i.e. holder of a share) in the important collegiate church of Pontesbury in Shropshire, where his brother Rees had once been the patron and lord.[51] And in July of 1326 the bishop of Hereford, Adam of Orleton, had taken the vacant church of Kinnersley into his own hands, and appointed Philip ap Hywel as one of two sequestrators to collect dues owing to him.[52]

Philip's position as a major landholder in Herefordshire, and his possession of the house of Hergest within Hereford diocese, together with his involvement as a portioner of Pontesbury church and as an episcopal officer, may lie behind an otherwise puzzling note in the margin of the Continuation of the Welsh chronicle *Brut y Tywysogion*. Next to the entry for 1329 in that text, are the now virtually illegible words, 'In that year died Master Philip at Hereford on the feast of Hilary and then he was buried in the burial place on the south side of the church.'[53] The problem with identifying this person with Philip ap Hywel is that the latter is not known to have had the title of Master.

But this may have been an honorific designation, or simply an error. There does not seem to be any other candidate for identification as the man whose death and burial are recorded in the margin of the chronicle text. The probability that that section of the chronicle was being written up in Valle Crucis or a major church in Maelor, and that it served as a continuation of *Brut y Tywysogion* seems to mark the man whose burial is recorded in 1329 as a Welshman. No member of the diocesan hierarchy of Hereford at that period is known to have been a Philip.[54] And Philip ap Hywel's territorial interests in Herefordshire as well as his position as archdeacon of Brecon (albeit in the diocese of St Davids) and his involvement in the clerical life of Hereford diocese were of sufficient significance to warrant a burial in an important place close to the cathedral church. There are no references to Philip ap Hywel as living after 1329, and so this enigmatic addition to the chronicle text would seem to be a record of the man whose career has been reconstructed here. Such a burial would have been particularly appropriate for a man whose life seems to have symbolised the late thirteenth and early fourteenth century March as a land of cultural transmission whose great families, principally of Norman descent but with increasing Welsh elements and associations, straddled the often porous zone of division between England and Wales.

In considering the career of Philip ap Hywel we should note that there are hints, and more than hints, that he continued that association with the families of Mortimer and de Bohun which had been so important to his father. Though his interests took him into the politics of England and Wales, Philip, again like his father, was above all a man of the March. A similar continuity with Hywel ap Meurig saw Philip maintain a particular interest in the land and castle of Builth. Philip ap Hywel seems not to have left children. His heir was his nephew, also called Philip, the son of his brother William.[55] Philip ap Hywel had developed significant landed interests, in Herefordshire and several other counties in England.[56] He shared many of these holdings with others, including his brother Rees, who himself was a prominent figure in the politics of the March and other parts of Wales, in a career which was perhaps even more successful, and more beset with danger, than Philip's. It is to Rees that we must now turn.

Notes

1 Edwards (ed.), *Littere Wallie*, p. 184.
2 Francis Jones, 'The subsidy of 1292', *BBCS* 13 (1950), p. 216.
3 There is an excellent summary of the episode in R. R. Davies, *Lordship and Society in the March of Wales 1282–1400* (Oxford: The Clarendon Press, 1978), pp. 268–9.
4 *AWR*, no. 457.
5 See Craig Owen Jones, *The Revolt of Madog ap Llywelyn* (Pwllheli: Llygad Gwalch, 2008), pp. 141–2. The observation at p. 141 that 'with the sole exception of Abergavenny, every castle assaulted by Morgan was owned by the Clare family, or had been constructed by Gloucester or one of his ancestors' needs to be amended as Abergavenny was certainly attacked not by Morgan but by the leader of the Gwentian rebels, Meurig ap Dafydd. See Stephenson, *Medieval Wales*, pp. 31, 165 n. 100, 183 n. 20.
6 See J. G. Edwards, 'The treason of Thomas Turberville', in R. W. Hunt et al. (eds), *Studies in Medieval History presented to Frederick Maurice Powicke* (Oxford: The Clarendon Press, 1948), pp. 296–309.
7 J. Beverley Smith, 'Edward II and the allegiance of Wales', *Welsh History Review*, 8 (1976–7), 139–71 at 142 n. 16.
8 Edwards, *Calendar of Ancient Correspondence*, p. 101.
9 *Calendar of Patent Rolls 1292–1301*, pp. 290–1. It is significant that the name of John de Lingeyne, a member of the family whose representatives had once ranked far higher than Hywel ap Meurig and his father (see, for examples: Smith, 'The Middle March', pp. 89–93; *Calendar of Liberate Rolls, 1251–60*, p. 480; *Close Rolls, 1259–61*, p. 310; *Close Rolls, 1261–64*, p. 136) now came below that of Philip ap Hywel.
10 *Parliamentary Writs and Writs of Military Summons*, p. 602.
11 John Webb (ed.), *A Roll of the Household Expenses of Richard de Swinfield, Bishop of Hereford, 1289–90* (London: Camden Society, 1854), p. 88.
12 *Calendar of Fine Rolls, Edward I, 1272–1307*, p. 423.
13 *Calendar of Fine Rolls, Edward 1307–19*, p. 46.
14 *Calendar of Patent Rolls, 1292–1301*, p. 598.
15 *Calendar of Close Rolls, 1307–13*, p. 3.
16 Ibid.
17 *Calendar of Patent Rolls, 1307–13*, p. 82.
18 *Calendar of Close Rolls, 1307–13*, p. 77.
19 *Calendar of Fine Rolls, 1307–19*, p. 58.
20 *Calendar of Patent Rolls, 1307–10*, p. 213.
21 See p. 58.
22 *Calendar of Close Rolls, 1307–13*, p. 52.
23 Ibid., p. 246.

24 Ibid.
25 *Calendar of Fine Rolls, 1307–19*, p. 58.
26 Ibid., p. 76.
27 Ibid., p. 188.
28 See David Stephenson, 'Crisis and Continuity in a Fourteenth-Century Welsh Lordship: The Struggle for Powys, 1312–32', *Cambrian Medieval Celtic Studies* (2013), 57–78.
29 *Calendar of Fine Rolls, 1307–19*, p. 188.
30 The record on the Patent Roll seems to suggest a pattern of tit-for-tat accusations, first noting 'the persons of the town of Builth in Wales and of the king's land there, who have committed assaults and other trespasses on the men of the king's castle of Builth and also upon his bailiffs and ministers there' – a case perhaps of Charlton getting his retaliation in first. This is then followed immediately by the record of a complaint by the commonalty of the land of Builth in Wales that the men of the king's castle of Builth and also of the king's bailiffs and ministers there have committed assaults and other trespasses and injuries upon them: *Calendar of Patent Rolls, 1307–19*, p. 322.
31 Ibid., p. 318.
32 In the study of the 'Celtic alliance', papers by J. Beverley Smith are of fundamental importance: see his 'Gruffudd Llwyd and the Celtic Alliance', *BBCS*, 26 (1974–6), 463–78, and 'Edward II and the allegiance of Wales', *Welsh History Review*, 8 (1976–7), 139–71.
33 *Calendar of Close Rolls, 1313–18*, p. 253.
34 See the king's order (ibid.) to the bishops, abbots etc. of north Wales to give credence to John de Grey, Philip and Rees in what they shall inform them on the king's behalf, and to execute what they shall direct.
35 Ibid., p. 270.
36 *Calendar of Patent Rolls, 1313–17*, p. 491.
37 There is a large literature on the events of 1321; see in particular J. Conway Davies, 'The Despenser war in Glamorgan', *Transactions of the Royal Historical Society*, 3rd Series, 9 (1915), 21–64. For the background, see Seymour Phillips, *Edward II* (London: Yale University Press, 2011), pp. 373–80.
38 *Calendar of Patent Rolls, 1321–24*, p. 18; also recorded (ibid.) is the pardon of Philip's nephew and heir, Philip de Clanvowe. See also the Appendix at pp. 123–6.
39 Phillips, *Edward II*, pp. 394–409.
40 The list of those to be arrested is particularly interesting. As well as Master Rees ap Hywel and Philip, his brother, it includes one certain near relation, their nephew Philip de Clanvowe, for whom see Chapter 5 below, and one man who may well be a (relatively young) grandson of Master Rees, Ieuan

ap Reys ap Maistre Reys. It is possible that the name has been copied in error and that we are dealing with a son of Master Rees. The likelihood of there being two men who could be described as Master Rees in a relatively narrow circle of opponents of the king in the Middle March seems fairly remote. In addition, the list includes two men, Meurig ap Rees and William ap 'Roys' his brother, who may also have been members of the family. See *Calendar of Patent Rolls, 1321–24*, p. 77, and see the Appendix below, at pp. 125–6.

41   These included Richard de Baskerville, Maurice ap Rhys (=Meurig ap Rees), Philip and John Havard, Hywel ap Dafydd, John and Philip Parpoynt, John le Receiver. See the following note.

42   *Calendar of Close Rolls, 1318–23*, p. 458.

43   Ibid., p. 582.

44   For Philip as a surety see *Calendar of Fine Rolls, 1319-27*, pp. 156 (with others, for Hywel ap Hywel), 161 (with Philip Joce, for Simon de Solers), 163 (with Nicholas de Hoperton, Yorks, for Richard de Pederton of Somerset). It has been suggested that Hywel ap Hywel may have been a member of the same family as Philip: see Siddons, *Development of Welsh Heraldry*, II, p. 456, sub Pouuel, Sire Ouuel, where his arms (Paly Or and Azure on a bend Gules three mullets Argent) are 'perhaps a differenced version of those of Hywel ap Meurig'. But an alternative identification has been made by Rees Davies, *Lordship and Society*, p. 225, where it is suggested that Hywel Fychan, grandson of Einion Sais of Brecon and thus a member of another powerful family of the Middle March, 'was almost certainly the Hywel ap Hywel of Wales'. This latter identification is based on the assumption that the man who appears as Hywel ap Hywel in record sources in, say, 1317 is the same man who, as Hywel Fychan (where 'Fychan' represents 'Junior') ap Hywel, appears (*Calendar of Fine Rolls, 1356–68*, p. 173) as a custodian of the de Bohun lordship of Brecon in 1361. It is possible that we are dealing with two similarly, though perhaps not identically, named men.

45   M. C. Jones, *The Feudal Barons of Powys* (London, 1868), p. 47.

46   Stephenson, 'Crisis and continuity', p. 62.

47   Jones, *Feudal Barons*, p. 16. It is however possible that the appearance of Charlton's name in this context represents an error, as he was not formally pardoned until September.

48   Roy Martin Haines, *King Edward II: His Life, His Reign, and its Aftermath, 1284–1330* (Montreal: McGill-Queen's University Press, 2003), p. 184.

49   *Calendar of Close Rolls, 1318–23*, p. 420: order of 14 February to the sheriff of Staffordshire to restore John Hinckley's lands. The Mortimers had surrendered on 22 January.

50   See p. 32, note 72.

51 *Calendar of Fine Rolls 1307–19*, p. 37, recording the 1309 grant of Pontesbury manor complete with advowsons of churches, by Rees ap Hywel to the king.

52 A. T. Bannister (ed.), *Registrum Ade de Orleton, Episcopi Herefordensis* (London: Canterbury and York Society, 1908), p. 366.

53 *BT Pen20* p. 126 n. 1. Dr Ian Bass (Personal comm.) suggests to me that it may be possible to identify Master Philip's burial place: 'he would have been buried in the Bishop's Cloister, the cloister which connected the bishop's palace and chapel with the nave of the cathedral … somewhere in the vicinity of the eastern range of the bishop's cloister … or in the Lady Arbour itself.'

54 The closest (though hardly convincing) candidate from within the diocesan hierarchy is one Master Philip Talbot who was archdeacon of Shropshire, but at a significantly earlier date than 1329. See J. S. Barrow (ed.), *Fasti Ecclesiae Anglicanae, vol. 8: Hereford*, p. 29, for Philip Talbot's collation to the archdeaconry of Shropshire in 1300, but at p. 55 it is suggested that he was dead by Apr. 1309 when his successor as archdeacon of Shropshire was recorded in office. In Joyce M. Horn (ed.), *Fasti Ecclesiae Anglicanae, vol 2: Hereford 1300–1541*, pp. 6–7 it is noted that Philip Talbot also occurs as archdeacon of Shropshire in 1303, but there is no further reference to him. It would seem unlikely that Philip Talbot, apparently a man without significant Welsh associations, would have been memorialised in a Welsh chronicle, and even less likely, given his disappearance from the records in the first decade of the fourteenth century, that he was the man whose death was recorded in 1329.

55 This Philip appears to have been the first member of the family to have adopted the Anglicised name 'de Clanvowe'. See below, pp. 69–70.

56 For discussion, see pp. 111–12 below.

4

The Empire Builders:
Master Rees ap Hywel and His Sons

i. Involvement in royal and Marcher government

Though they sometimes worked together and had interests in common, the careers of Philip ap Hywel and his brother Master Rees ap Hywel were very different, with different outcomes. Rees appears in governmental records significantly later than Philip and may have been some years younger than him. It has been asserted that Rees was inducted to the parish of Kington, which included his brother's house at Hergest, as early as 1287. This, however, was far from certain. All that we can say with confidence is that he was ordained as a subdeacon, the lowest of the major orders of the Church, in the diocese of Hereford in that year.[1]

By 1301 Rees was involved in the work of the government; in June of that year he was appointed, along with his brother Philip and Walter de Pederton, the deputy justiciar of south Wales, as a paymaster for troops from south and west Wales about to go on campaign for the king in Scotland.[2] In that record he is already described as Master Rees, and this indicates that he had studied both the trivium and the quadrivium in university. This may help to explain his absence from government records before that date. By 1302 Master Rees was also involved in the administration of the lands of Humphrey de Bohun, 4th earl of Hereford. In that year Earl Humphrey married Elizabeth, daughter of Edward I, and as part of the marriage arrangements Earl Humphrey surrendered all his lands and the earldoms of Hereford and Essex to the king, who granted them back entailed on the earl and his bride. During the initial surrender of the earl's lands, it was reported that at the castle and lordship of Caldecot in Gwent, Master Rees ap Hywel delivered possession to the king's officers on behalf of the earl.[3] He was thus already in a responsible position in Humphrey's service.

In 1305 he can be found acting in the service of the king's son, Edward of Caernarfon, then prince of Wales.[4] In the following years some of the records which mention Rees relate to his acquisition of lands, a subject which will be investigated below. But it is clear that he was mixing with senior government officials and that he was being employed in important business. Thus in 1309 he was commissioned, once more with Walter de Pederton, the deputy Justiciar, and Master William Hore to hold inquisitions into the sensitive issue of office-holding in west Wales.[5] In 1312 Master Rees was appointed deputy Justiciar of South Wales.[6] Though he held the post for only a few months he was the first Welshman to occupy this crucial position in the government of the south.

We have already noted that in 1315 Rees joined his brother Hywel and Master John Walwayn in preparing both north and south Wales to resist any attempt by Edward Bruce and his allies in Ireland to invade Wales.[7] The following year he undertook a task of similar sensitivity. Again, he was associated with John Walwayn, this time in collecting fines levied on those who had been involved in the recent rebellion in the lands of the late Gilbert de Clare, earl of Gloucester and lord of Glamorgan.[8] This relates to the rebellion of the Welsh lord Llywelyn Bren, a movement which had received widespread sympathy, even among Llywelyn's opponents.[9] The collection of fines for involvement was therefore a delicate task. It would appear that by 1316 Master Rees was taking his place with his brother Philip in the government and politics of much of Wales. The brothers were beginning to rival vastly influential figures like Sir Gruffudd Llwyd, descendant of Llywelyn the Great's steward Ednyfed Fychan and a stalwart of royal governance in the north. But as was the case with Philip ap Hywel, Rees seems to disappear from the government records for several years after 1316. It is likely that he followed Roger Mortimer and Humphrey de Bohun into opposition to the king, but it is difficult to trace the stages by which this process unfolded.

Roy Martin Haines, discussing the period after 1316, notes that Rees 'subsequently took service with Mortimer of Wigmore, and, more particularly, with Hereford. Despenser [Hugh the Younger] was well aware of his activities and in a letter to John Yweyn (Inge), his sheriff of Glamorgan, suggested that it might be prudent to secure a commission to apprehend Rhys [sic, for the more usual Rees].'[10] But the letter to which Haines refers can be identified as one written by Despenser (the royal favourite, and target of the anger of the Marcher lords) on 18 January 1321.[11] What the letter does reveal is the extent to which Rees had emerged as a significant force in the politics of south-east Wales, for it notes that 'Master Rhys ap Hywel makes fresh alliances, and leads a great rout of people with him.'

ii. Rebellion and imprisonment

As well as undertaking numerous governmental tasks it seems that Rees had been making energetic moves to build up a large lordship of his own within Wales. This becomes clear in the records for the early 1320s. January of 1321 saw a royal order to the Justiciar of Wales, Roger Mortimer of Chirk, soon to fall dramatically from office, to take Master Rees ap Hywel and bring him in front of the king, as it had been found by an inquisition conducted by Hugh Despenser the elder that Rees was 'one of the principal abettors and maintainers of those who had by force of arms' prevented a royal official from taking the land of Gower into the king's hands by virtue of the king's order.[12] The background to this event was that the lordship of Gower had become debated territory after its lord, William de Braose, had given it to his son-in-law John de Mowbray without royal permission. Hugh Despenser the younger had persuaded the king to take possession of Gower, and to appoint him as the keeper of the lordship. Rees ap Hywel appears to have coordinated and led the opposition to the royal seizure of the lordship. As such, he was in grave danger.

But as the baronial opposition to King Edward gathered momentum in 1321 Master Rees appears to have become more deeply implicated in resistance to Edward and the Despensers. At the time of the baronial ascendancy and the (temporary) exile of the Despensers, we have seen that pardons were issued to the king's leading opponents. Like his brother Philip, Master Rees was one of those pardoned, in August 1321.[13] But that of course was a situation which would soon be reversed. In January of 1322, the time of the king's offensive against his baronial opponents and the surrender to him of the Mortimers, the following dramatic order was issued. It was addressed to the people of

the castles, towns lands and lordships following, to wit, the castle of Dolforwyn and the lands of Ceri and Cedewain, the castles of Dinboeth and Cefnllys and the lands there, the lands of Maelienydd and Gwerthrynion, the castle, town and lands of Builth, the castle, town and lands of Brecknock, the castles and towns of Huntington and Hay, and the lands there, the castles and lands of Bwlchydinas, Blaenllyfni and Pencelli, the castle and town of Bronllys and the lands there and the lands of Cantref Selyf, and the castle, town and lands of Crickhowell and Ystrad Yw, to be intendant [obedient] to Gruffudd ap Rhys whom the king has appointed to take into the king's hand the said castles and all the lands of Roger Mortimer of Wigmore, Humphrey de Bohun earl of Hereford and Essex, Roger Mortimer of Chirk, Master Rees ap Hywel and Amauri de Pauncefoot …'[14]

A little later comes the precise instruction to Gruffudd ap Rhys (i.e. Sir Gruffudd Llwyd) to hand over to Richard le Marshal the castle and town of Bronllys and the lands there and the lands of Cantref Selyf and the goods and chattels of Master Rees ap Hywel therein.[15] What is remarkable in these documents is the fact that Rees was being treated not simply as a follower of the Marcher lords who had surrendered or were soon to be brought to disastrous battle, but as a fellow Marcher, the lord of Bronllys and Cantref Selyf.

The process of seizure of Master Rees's assets was remarkably thorough. In the lordship of Usk a manor, which Maud, wife of the late Gilbert de Clare earl of Gloucester and Hertford, had held in wardship for the daughters of the dead tenant, had been assigned to the custody of Master Rees ap Hywel for the duration of the minority of the heiresses for an annual payment of £20. The countess had subsequently died, and her executors received the payments which she had directed should be spent for the good of her soul. But the record of the arrangement, dated 2 June 1322, notes that the manor is now in the king's hand, because of the forfeiture of Master Rees.[16]

And while his lands and even his goods and chattels were being seized, where was Rees himself? By 12 March 1322 he was a prisoner in Dover Castle, where the constable was ordered to provide him with sufficient maintenance for himself and a chamberlain.[17] And for greater security at some point he was transferred to the Tower of London to which his former lords and allies the Mortimers had been consigned. It was perhaps in recognition of his rise to power and celebrity that he was accorded residence in the Tower, the ultimate and often fatal place of confinement of the once great of the realm. Master Rees was a captive for over four years. His life must have been endangered when Roger Mortimer of Wigmore escaped from the Tower in 1323, and even though he was not executed, he was lucky to avoid the fate of Roger Mortimer of Chirk, another of the prisoners in the Tower, who died in August of 1326, a month before a vengeful Mortimer of Wigmore, accompanied by his lover Queen Isabella, invaded England.[18]

iii. Freedom and triumph

Rees survived his imprisonment and was rapidly restored to his freedom and his possessions as Mortimer took control of the realm. Indeed, Master Rees wasted no time in gaining the approval of the new regime by taking a leading part in the hunting down of the fleeing Edward II in November 1326. One of the chronicles of Edward II's reign, the *Vita et Mors Edwardi Secundi* (Life and Death of Edward II) records what happened:

> The queen, staying at Hereford, divided her army, and sent with one part of it Henry, the earl of Leicester and Master Rees ap Hywel, a clerk of Welsh nationality, to capture the king and those with him. The afore-mentioned earl was the kinsman and heir of Thomas, earl of Lancaster, and that Rees who was sent with him had been imprisoned by royal order in the Tower of London but had been restored to liberty by the queen's power. Both the aforesaid earl and Rees had possessions and large lordships close to the place where the king was hiding. The whole

region was very well known to Rees. Then the earl and the clerk, having employed money to bribe some of the Welsh, found out through Welsh scouts that the king and Hugh Despenser the younger had been deserted by their supporters who had taken flight, and were in the monastery of Neath. The king and Hugh, Robert Baldock and Simon Reading were thus captured ...[19]

It is likely that the actual capture was effected as Edward and his party were attempting to make for the Despenser castle of Llantrisant. Now Rees hastened to restore his position as a lord of the March and as a landholder in several parts of Wales and the borderland. He petitioned the new king, Edward III, whose reign was reckoned from 25 January 1327 soon after his father's abdication on 21 January. The petition is much damaged and is undated but clearly belongs to the early part of 1327. Rees prays that our lord the King 'may grant delivery of his lands and tenements with fees and advowsons (the right of presentation of clergy to churches) ...with arrears arising therefrom ... and that he may have his goods and chattels which he finds have been carried off ...'[20] The response was crisp and positive: 'Let this petition be sent to the chancery, and let the chancellor inform himself of the reason why the lands and other things ... were taken into the king's hand; and if they were taken by reason of the quarrel [of the barons with the king] and not for another reason let the lands, tenements, fees and advowsons be restored with the issues and arrears ...'[21] By late February the restoration of lands to Master Rees in Blaenllyfni, Usk, Gower and Brecon was announced in the Parliament Roll.[22] The lands in Brecon to which he was restored included the large lordship of Bronllys with Cantref Selyf, held of the earl of Hereford. It is clear that he was also reinstated in his lordship of Talgarth.

Other marks of the favour of the new regime were evident. As early as November 1326 he had been granted several ecclesiastical preferments, including the prebend of Shipton in the diocese of Salisbury and the prebend of Finsbury in that of St Paul's.[23] At about the same time he had been entrusted with the custody of the castle and lands of Builth, which had been held by Humphrey de Bohun before his death at Boroughbridge.[24] This period of control of lands which had long been associated with his family came to an end in February of 1327 when he was required to hand them over to the new earl of Hereford, John de Bohun. A still greater office had been conferred on him in November 1326, when he was appointed Justiciar of South Wales.[25] He had previously held the deputy Justiciarship, as had the towering figure of Sir Rhys ap Gruffudd, but Master Rees ap Hywel was the first Welsh incumbent of the post of Justiciar, a clear sign of his status in the eyes of the English government.

Rees was not to hold the post of Justiciar for long. He appears to have been an interim holder between the execution in November 1326 of the previous Justiciar, Edmund FitzAlan, earl of Arundel, and the arrival of the triumphant and covetous Roger Mortimer of Wigmore, who took both the southern and northern Justiciarships in February 1327. But any disappointment Rees may have felt at this was surely dispelled by his restoration to his lands and lordships in the same month, as well, perhaps as by an order issued to the chamberlain of south Wales in February to pay to Master Rees lately the king's Justice in South Wales and West Wales the arrears for the accustomed fee for that office for the time when he was Justice.[26] And he continued to be appointed to powerful posts. In his last days as Justiciar he was selected to investigate suspected offences committed by royal officers – under the regime of Edward II and the Despensers – in South and West Wales and in the lordship of Montgomery.[27] In July of the same year he was commissioned to inspect and report on the condition of the royal castles in South Wales, a task in which he seems to have acted with considerable efficiency, reporting on defects found at Dryslwyn in the Tywi valley.[28] As the appointments continued, so did the ecclesiastical rewards: by 11 April 1328 Rees had received a grant of a prebend in St Davids.[29] He did not live long to enjoy this last appointment, for by late May he was dead.[30] Cleric or not, Master Rees left many children, and one of them, Philip, became his heir.[31]

iv. Master Rees's legacy

We have seen that Master Rees gathered into his hands a collection of ecclesiastical benefices in his last years, in several dioceses. But what is more striking is his very significant accumulation of secular lordships.

It seems clear that Rees had manoeuvred to secure the whole of the lordship of Talgarth by surrendering to the king the Shropshire manor of Pontesbury which he had acquired in 1305.[32] In February of 1309 the successful outcome of his plans was recorded on the government's Charter Roll, where there was noted:

> the grant to Rees ap Hywel and his heirs, in consideration of his surrender to the king of the manor of Pontesbury, county of Shropshire, of the reversion of all the lands in the manor of Talgarth in the Marches of Wales, which John son of Reginald lately quit-claimed to the king and which the king afterwards restored to the said John to hold for life with reversion to the king, to be held with the park, pasture, mill and its suits, services and all other appurtenances, as freely as the said John held them and for the same services.[33]

It would seem that once granted his lands back, John fitz Reginald had made them over to Rees with royal licence. John's death in 1310 had simplified the situation, as it left Rees as the clear holder of Talgarth in its entirety, saving only a claim for dower by John's widow Agnes.[34]

The complex story of Talgarth continued down to the death of Rees, when an inquisition heard that there had been further developments after he had acquired the manor in 1309. It recorded that Rees had held the manor, 'and gave it in fee and inheritance to William ap Rees [a near relation?] who held the same for a year and more;[35] and afterwards the said William, with the king's licence, gave the manor to Rees ap Hywel, Philip ap Hywel and Philip de Bronllys, to hold to them and the heirs of the body of the said Philip de Bronllys, of the king in chief [i.e. as hereditary tenants of the king] by homage only, and by giving aid against the Welsh in time of war in Wales , as other like tenants do for keeping the peace; with successive remainders in tail to his brothers John, Rees and James, and Elizabeth his sister, with reversion to the right heirs of the said Rees ap Hywel [i.e. in the event of failure of heirs to Philip de Bronllys, the estate would pass to John, and in the event of failure of heirs of John, to Rees, and so on] for all which the said charter of King Edward II was shown. And the said Philip and Philip, jointly with the said Rees, held the said manor until the death of the said Rees, since when the said manor has been in the king's hand' [i.e. against the terms of the entail detailed in the inquisition report; it should have passed to Philip of Bronllys, and eventually it did].[36] The irony of the provision that the tenant of Talgarth should give aid against the Welsh in time of war is striking. It possibly originates in a period when it must have been thought impossible that the lord might be Welsh, or alternatively it may suggest that 'Welsh' was sometimes used not as an ethnic descriptor, but as a sign of political allegiance.[37]

Philip of Bronllys is clearly to be identified as a son of Master Rees often called, in traditional Welsh fashion, Philip ap Rees. But his 'frenchified' designation as Philip de Bronllys, reveals that his father had acquired at some stage the important castle and lordship of Bronllys, together with the adjacent Cantref Selyf. It is not entirely clear when the acquisition was made. In the later decades of the thirteenth century Bronllys and Cantref Selyf were in the hands of the Giffards as tenants of the de Bohun lord of Brecon. But after the death of John Giffard in 1299 this portion of his widespread lands passed to an heiress, his daughter Maud. She died in 1311, and it cannot have been long before these territories were acquired by Master Rees, for this was, as we have seen, the period of his greatest eminence as an administrator for Edward II.[38]

Like Talgarth, Bronllys and Cantref Selyf were part of the inheritance of Philip ap Rees. It is evident that Master Rees held lands in other parts of Wales – in Usk, in Blaenllyfni and in Gower – and even in England. He seems to have held several manors in Herefordshire and Worcestershire as a co-tenant with his brother Philip, and often with a third co-tenant.[39] These jointly held lands were not negligible: those held by the brothers with Joan Pychard amounted to four-and -a-half knights' fees, while those held with Richard de la Lynde were reckoned at two-and-three-quarters knights' fees. Though most of his associates were English officials and gentry and some at least of his lands were in England, Master Rees was frequently involved in administrative and political matters in Wales and the March, and was indeed a Marcher lord in his own right. With Master Rees ap Hywel the family of Meurig ap Philip had reached new heights of esteem, power and wealth as well as the insecurity that such things so often brought. His eminence was a challenge to the next generation.

v. Philip ap Rees the Marcher lord and his brothers

We have seen that of Master Rees ap Hywel's several sons, one of them, Philip, was clearly his principal heir. But some of the others were by no means negligible figures. Ieuan (John) ap Rees was an adherent of Humphrey de Bohun, earl of Hereford, in the crisis of 1321 and 1322 and was amongst those whose arrest was sought by royal officers in February of the latter year.[40] Ieuan can probably be identified as the Ieuan ap Rees who was recorded as deputy Justiciar of South Wales in 1337 presiding over an enquiry into payments to the steward, constables and other officers of Blaenllyfni and Bwlchydinas.[41] Two years later Ieuan ap Rees was deputy to Hugh Tyrel, keeper of the manor of Radnor.[42] He is certainly the Ieuan ap Rees ap Hywel who was associated in the same year with his kinsman Philip de Clanvowe and with Edmund Hakelut to survey the estate of Sir Rhys ap Gruffudd at Lampeter.[43] In 1340 he was steward of the Mortimer lordships, thus continuing a long tradition in his family.[44] Thereafter he seems to disappear from royal records. Rees ap Rees, a younger brother of Philip ap Rees, was significant enough for Philip to grant him the reversion of his estates in 1352.[45] By the time of Philip's death he seems also to have been dead.

But it is with Philip ap Rees that we are principally concerned. The heir to Talgarth, Bronllys and Cantref Selyf was effectively a Marcher lord in his own right – and his dignity was emphasised in his designation on occasion as Philip de Bronllys. He was a knight, but the date of his knighting is unclear.[46] Philip ap Rees may not have been as prominent in royal administration as his father had been.[47] But he was commissioned in 1335 to raise five hundred men for Edward III from the de Bohun lordships of Brecon, Hay, Huntingdon and Cantref Selyf, in the last of which he was the earl's tenant.[48] In 1342 he was appointed, together with Rhys ap Gruffudd, Thomas of Castle Goodrich, chamberlain of South Wales, and Richard de Southorpe, to 'take the final account of all bailiffs, ministers, farmers and keepers of castles, manors, towns and lands which were in the custody of Roger Mortimer, late earl of March and John Mautravers, lately in the king's hands, who are bound to render account and who have not yet done so, and to arrest any whom they find rebellious in the rendering accounts …'[49] But his subsequent service to the Crown raised problems of an ominous nature.

It appears that in 1343, and probably earlier, Philip ap Rees was the constable and keeper of the castle and lordship of Builth. He was therefore maintaining a connection with that lordship which was of long standing in his family. In that year the leading men of each region of Wales which was part of the territories of the newly installed prince of Wales, Edward the Black Prince, were required to assemble and to swear fealty to him. On the appointed day Philip ap Rees was absent, and was represented by his lieutenant, Owain ab Ieuan.[50] It is entirely possible, from the tenor of the report of events, that Philip was not a resident constable, and that his duties were normally discharged by Owain ab Ieuan. But Owain too absented himself when he knew that the king's officers were coming to Builth to exact the oaths of fealty. He left the castle in the charge of the janitor, Dafydd Goch, with instructions not to allow the royal officers to enter the castle. When the officers arrived, they were duly refused admission, but they took Dafydd and imprisoned him until he allowed them into the castle. The officers promptly took the castle and lordship into the king's hand and handed it over to Sir Rhys ap Gruffudd to hold until further instructions were received. Owain ab Ieuan was found by Sir Rhys ap Gruffudd and obliged to find sureties that he would answer to the king or the prince for his act of contempt.[51] Whether Sir Philip ap Rees was behind the attempt to deny access to the king's officers is unknown, but he appears to have been relieved of his offices at Builth. It is evident that Philip was unlikely to be regarded as a dutiful custodian of this important lordship, and it is possible that the episode marked the end of his official career.

It was, however, the events of the previous year that were to prove even more ominous. In 1342 Philip was commissioned first to raise two hundred men from Pencelli, Blaenllyfni and Cantref Selyf.[52] But Humphrey de Bohun objected that Pencelli and Cantref Selyf were his lordships, so that he should be the one to raise troops from them. The result of de Bohun's intervention was that Philip and his associated commissioner Miles Pychard were required only to raise troops from Blaenllyfni. It is clear that de Bohun was sensitive to the issue of who was actually responsible for Cantref Selyf. His view was that as the overlord he should be the one to raise troops rather than his tenant, Philip ap Rees. The issue of control of Cantref Selyf had been raised, and once raised it would not go away. It arose again in 1347 when Earl Humphrey was ordered to raise two hundred men from his lordship of Brecon. He clearly understood this to mean from the parts of the lordship under his direct control and those which were subject to an intermediate lord, in this case Cantref Selyf under the lordship of Philip ap Rees. It appears that Earl Humphrey imprisoned six tenants of the lordship of Cantref Selyf on the grounds that they had not responded to a summons by the bailiff of Brecon to participate in an array for military service which had been ordered by the king; the six men claimed that they were to answer to the bailiffs of Cantref Selyf, and that the only occasion when they were answerable to the bailiff of Brecon was in the event of the failure of the Cantref Selyf bailiff to obey the royal command. After negotiations between the earl and Philip ap Rees an agreement of sorts was concluded in October of 1348, but it was clear that Earl Humphrey was not going to stop in his determination to establish his control over Cantref Selyf.[53]

Matters came to a head in 1349. Sir Philip was summoned to Earl Humphrey's court to face quo warranto proceedings.[54] These required him to prove by what warrant (*Quo warranto*) he claimed to have cognisance of a vast range of pleas, including pleas of the Crown, in his lordship and the right to pardon convicted persons as well as to seize the chattels of his tenants in the lordship even if they were convicted outside his lands. There was nothing particularly unusual about Earl Humphrey's campaign to extinguish the claims to quasi-regal powers of an intermediate lord: the same thing was taking place in many regions of the March. And the outcome of the proceedings against Philip was inevitable: he was found guilty of usurping the powers and rights of his lord the earl of Hereford, and by 1351 his lands of Bronllys and Cantref Selyf were confiscated.[55]

The chief beneficiary of this process was Earl Humphrey's avaricious brother, William de Bohun, Earl of Northampton, who took over Philip's lordship of Bronllys and Cantref Selyf. Even his entirely separate lordship of Talgarth was eroded. The reality of the situation was made clear in an entry on the Patent Roll in June of 1352, recording:

a licence for William de Bohun, earl of Northampton, to grant to Philip ap Rees, knight, and Joan his wife, in tail, the manor of Ideshale (Shifnall), held in chief (an acre of land and the advowson of the church of the manor excepted) with remainders to the heirs of the body of the said Philip, to Rees ap Rees and the heirs of his body, to John Bluet, son and heir to Elizabeth Bluet[56] and the heirs of his body, and to the right heirs of the said Philip. Grant also that if the manors of Bronllys and Llangoed, the land of Cantref Selyf, the park of Talgarth, sixty acres of land, thirty acres of meadow and ten acres of moor in Talgarth, which the earl has of the grant of Philip and Joan, or any parcel thereof, by plea or other process in the king's court at the suit of the same Philip and Joan or their heirs or by heirs of the said Philip, or by the said Rees and John or their heirs, be recovered out of the hands of the earl or his heirs, without their fault, it shall be lawful for them to re-enter into the manor of Ideshale or such part thereof as is to the value of the manors and lands recovered from them.[57]

And yet the situation might have been worse. There was after all some recompense as it is clear that Earl William had made over to Philip by way of exchange for some of his forced acquisitions the rich Shropshire manor of Shifnall.[58] Sir Philip ap Rees would still die a member of the gentry class with lands in both the March and England, worth some £150 per year, even if he was not the major lord that he had once been.[59]

We have seen that such 'consolidation' of a lordship by a great magnate at the expense of intermediate lords was not an unusual process in the March. But it is possible that there was a little more to it than just rapacity on the part of the de Bohun brothers. One of the distinct features of the surviving great tower of Bronllys castle is what seems to be either an addition of a top storey or a complete rebuild. The quality of the stonework and of the facilities of the upper storey is far superior to that of the earlier lower parts of the tower, and a number of very unwarlike and decorative windows have been inserted into the building. The refined improvements to the structure seem clearly to have been done in the fourteenth century, and current opinion is undecided as to whether it was the work of Master Rees or his son Philip of Bronllys.[60] The new features seem to sit more comfortably with the period of Sir Philip. Rees was the busier man in terms of official assignments, and much of his later life was spent in prison or trying to restore his position on his release. Philip on the other hand was much less occupied with official assignments and had the resources and the time to conduct a campaign of rebuilding. If that is correct, then it may well have acted as an additional spur to action on the part of Earl Humphrey when he knew that his vassal Philip was making a political statement of his permanence in Bronllys by improving the castle in a way that transformed it from a military structure into a lordly residence.

Philip ap Rees died in August 1369. His brothers were all dead. His inquisition post mortem recorded that he left as heirs to his lands held in chief, Talgarth English and Shifnall, his daughters Elizabeth and Mabel.[61] Elizabeth had been married to Sir Henry Mortimer, but he had died, and she had remarried, to Adam Peasenhall. Mabel died some six weeks after her father. She had a son Hugh, who died a few weeks after his mother, leaving her husband, Sir Hugh Wrottesley, to pursue a claim to part of the inheritance.[62] But the Talgarth estate was later inherited by a descendant of Elizabeth Bluet, daughter of Rees ap Rees, and therefore Sir Philip's niece.[63] And so Talgarth and Shifnal passed into other hands, with the extinction of the male line of Rees ap Hywel ap Meurig. But one line of Hywel ap Meurig's descendants was to be more enduring, and to enjoy great fame and achievement. These were the descendants of William ap Hywel.

Notes

1   W. W. Capes (ed.), *Registrum Ricardi de Swinfield* (London: Canterbury and York Society, 1909), p. 548. There is discussion in Smith, 'Marcher regality', p. 269 n. 7, where it is noted that 'the institution is not recorded in the printed edition of Swinfield's register ... but the editor of the household roll (*Household Expenses*, p. 88) refers to the institution, quoting the register as his authority.' It seems that we are compelled to regard the institution of Rees as an error.

2   *Parliamentary Writs*, p. 602.

3   *Calendar of Inquisitions, Miscellaneous*, II, p. 508.

4   Hilda Johnstone (ed.), *Letters of Edward of Caernarfon, 1284–1307* (Manchester University Press, 1946), p. 141.

5   *Calendar of Inquisitions, Miscellaneous*, II, pp. 18–19.

6   Ralph A. Griffiths, *The Principality of Wales in the Late Middle Ages: The Structure and Personnel of Government. I, South Wales 1277–1536* (Cardiff: University of Wales Press, 1972), p. 97.

7   See above, pp. 38–9.

8   Natalie Fryde (ed.), *List of Welsh Entries in the Memoranda Rolls 1282–1343* (Cardiff: University of Wales Press, 1974), p. 40.

9   See Craig Owen Jones, *Llywelyn Bren* (Llanrwst: Gwasg Carreg Gwalch, 2006), pp. 69–70.

10 Haines, *King Edward II*, p. 122. The comment that Rees had taken service with Hereford after 1316 may distort the situation somewhat, as it is noted by Griffiths, *Principality of Wales*, p. 98 that he had been in Hereford's service since at least 1302.

11 Edwards, *Calendar of Ancient Correspondence*, pp. 219–20.

12 *Calendar of Close Rolls, 1318–23*, p. 285.

13 Griffiths, *Principality of Wales*, p. 98.

14 *Calendar of Fine Rolls, 1319–27*, p. 91.

15 Ibid., p. 92.

16 *Calendar of Inquisitions, Miscellaneous*, II, p. 123; compare *Calendar of Charter Rolls, 1300–26*, p. 451, for another forfeiture, of 'Stryflond' in Wales which passed to the king, and then to Hugh Despenser.

17 *Calendar of Close Rolls, 1318–23*, p. 427. The record suggests that his captivity in Dover Castle was not too onerous.

18 Mortimer of Chirk died on 3 August 1326; accounts of his burial vary – see Haines, *King Edward II*, p. 429 n. 21.

19 William Stubbs (ed.), *Chronicles of the Reigns of Edward I and Edward I*, vol. II (Rolls Series, London, 1883), p. 311 (my translation).

20 William Rees (ed.), *Calendar of Ancient Petitions relating to Wales* (Cardiff: University of Wales Press, 1975), p. 75.

21 Ibid.

22 *Rotuli Parliamentorum*, II, p. 423.

23 Joyce M. Horn (ed.), *Fasti Ecclesiae Anglicanae 1300–1541: vol. 3, Salisbury Diocese* (London, 1962), p. 84; eadem (ed.), *Fasti Ecclesiae Anglicanae 1300–1541: vol. 5, St Paul's, London* (London, 1963), p. 37.

24 *Calendar of the Memoranda Rolls, 1326–27*, p. 122.

25 Griffiths, *Principality of South Wales*, p. 102.

26 Ibid.

27 The commission of Oyer and Terminer was issued to Roger Mortimer, John de Bouser, Rees ap Hywel and Robert de Malley: *Calendar of Patent Rolls, 1327–30*, p. 72.

28 Natalie Fryde, *List of Welsh Entries in the Memoranda Rolls*, p. 71.

29 B. Jones (ed.), *Fasti Ecclesiae Anglicanae 1300–1541: vol. 11, the Welsh Dioceses (Bangor, Llandaff, St Asaph, St Davids)* (London, 1965), p. 80.

30 *Calendar of Patent Rolls, 1327–30*, p. 273.

31 See p. 58. See also *Calendar of Patent Rolls, 1307–13*, p. 458 where there is reference to Philip de Bronllys (Philip ap Rees), but also to John de Bronllys,

Rees de Bronllys and James de Bronllys, as well as to Master Rees's daughter Elizabeth de Bronllys.

[32] See Bridget Wells-Furby (ed.), *A Catalogue of the Medieval Muniments at Berkeley Castle*, 2 vols, Gloucestershire Record Series, vols 17 and 18 (Bristol and Gloucestershire Archaeological Society, 2004).

[33] *Calendar of Charter Rolls, 1300–1326*, p. 125.

[34] John's Inquisition Post Mortem in 1310 noted that 'the manor of Talgarth together with the hamlet of Neweton was held by Rees ap Hywel by the king's grant in exchange for the manor of Pontesbury in Shropshire of which manor of Talgarth the said John enfeoffed the king by his deed, who afterwards granted it to him for life, but a year before his death he delivered it to the said Rees by the king's licence.' *Calendar of Inquisitions Post Mortem, 1307–16*, p. 107. The same Inquisition reveals another aspect of Master Rees's acquisitiveness, for it mentions two cases in which he held lands of heirs who were in his wardship. The Inquisition also instructs the escheator to survey the lands formerly held by John in West Wales, Talgarth and Nether Gwent, on the petition of Agnes for her dower. It should also be noted that the entry in I. H. Jeayes, *Descriptive Catalogue of the Charters and Muniments in the Possession of Lord Fitzhardinge at Berkeley* Castle (Bristol, 1892), pp. 212–13, no. 718, which purports to be a licence of Edward VI to Rees ap Hywel, clerk, to enfeoff William ap Rees in Talgarth manor, and to the latter to grant the same to Philip ap Hywel, clerk, and to the said Rees and Philip de Bronllys is actually one of Edward II, in 1312. See Wells-Furby, *Catalogue of the Medieval Muniments at Berkeley Castle*, II, p. 668, (C2/2/6).

[35] See Appendix pp. 123–6 for discussion of whether William ap Rees may have been related to Rees ap Hywel.

[36] *Calendar of Inquisitions Post Mortem, 1327–36*, p. 143.

[37] A useful example of this relates to the history of Kinnerley on the Shropshire-Powys border. It had passed down since the twelfth century in the hands of a family descended from Iorwerth Goch, the brother of Madog ap Maredudd, the ruler of Powys. Eventually it passed into the possession of Gruffudd ap Madog, lord of Bromfield/Maelor, ruler of northern Powys, who held the land of Kinnerley on behalf of his kinsman by marriage, James Audley. Gruffudd held the manor 'until he was ejected by the force of the Welsh'. Gruffudd of course was Welsh. But he was an 'English' ally at the time when he was ejected by 'the Welsh'. *Welsh Assize Roll*, p. 249.

[38] R. R. Davies, *Lordship and Society*, p. 46 n. 41 very rightly noted that 'the story of the descent of the Giffard lands in the March is a complex one'. The precise point at which Bronllys and Cantref Selyf passed to Master Rees remains obscure; all that is attempted here is a reasonable guess.

[39] See below, p. 112 and notes 13–16.

[40] It is possible that the reference to 'Ievan ap Reys fitz Maistre Reys' whose arrest was sought in that month is an error for Ieuan fitz Maistre Rees. For discussion see note 40 at pp. 47–8.

[41] *Calendar of Inquisitions, Miscellaneous*, II, p. 379.

[42] Ibid., p. 404. The irony in this episode is that Ieuan was representing the keeper of Radnor, Hugh Tyrel, who was being held responsible for denying an annual fee of five ells of cloth to Ieuan's own kinsman, Philip de Clanvowe, whose complaints had triggered the inquisition, and with whom he was associated in survey of 1 April 1339, for which see the following note.

[43] *Calendar of Patent Rolls 1338–40*, p. 279.

[44] TNA, SC 6/1209/9; discussion by J. Beverley Smith, 'Marcher regality: Quo Warranto proceedings relating to Cantrefselyf in the lordship of Brecon, 1349', *BBCS*, 28 (1978–80), 267–88, at p. 270 n. 6.

[45] *Calendar of Patent Rolls, 1350–54*, pp. 261, 294.

[46] Philip's status as a knight is made clear in several documents; see, for example, references at p. 62.

[47] It appears, however, that until the mid-1340s, he was rather more prominent as a royal officer than is suggested by Beverley Smith, 'Marcher regality', p. 270.

[48] *Rotuli Scotie*, I, p. 332.

[49] *Calendar of Patent Rolls, 1340–43*, p. 450.

[50] *Original Documents produced as a supplement to the Archaeologia Cambrensis*, vol. 1, 1877, clxiv.

[51] Ibid., clxiv–clxv.

[52] Smith, 'Marcher regality', p. 271.

[53] Ibid., p. 272 et seq.

[54] Ibid. There is concise discussion in Davies, *Lordship and Society*, p. 97.

[55] Ibid.

[56] i.e. daughter of Rees ap Rees, and so niece of Philip ap Rees.

[57] *Calendar of Patent Rolls, 1350–54*, p. 294. It was presumably as part of the process of tidying up these arrangements that a quitclaim of Talgarth to Philip ap Rees was made by John de 'Clambow' in 1352 (Wells-Furby (ed.), *A Catalogue of the Medieval Muniments at Berkeley Castle*, p. 668 (C2/2/8). This looks very much like John de Clanvowe (d. 1361) who may thus have had an interest in Talgarth, which he was induced to surrender to Sir Philip. If so, it indicates that the two branches of the descendants of Hywel ap Meurig were still in contact. Compare the spelling 'Clambow' with the spelling of the name of Perryne, Sir Thomas Clanvowe's wife, in her will, wherein she appears as 'Clanbowe': p. 98 below.

[58] *Calendar of Patent Rolls, 1350–54*, p. 294.

[59] See the comments of Wells-Furby, *A Catalogue of the Medieval Muniments at Berkeley Castle*, II, p. 658.

[60] See Robert Scourfield and Richard Haslam, *The Buildings of Wales: Powys* (London: Yale University Press, 2013), pp. 454–5, especially the comment (p. 455) that 'around 1311 the castle came into the hands of a Welshman, Rhys ap Hywel, and at some stage in the early C14 the uppermost floor of the round keep was added, or perhaps totally rebuilt, and windows were altered on the lower floor; the work was of [sic] either by Rhys or his son Philip'. It is possible that even more of the evident alterations in the tower (noted ibid.) were of the same date.

[61] *Calendar of Inquisitions Post Mortem*, XII, no. 313, p. 286.

[62] Ibid.

[63] See the complex discussion in Wells-Furby, *A Catalogue of the Medieval Muniments at Berkeley Castle*, II, pp. 657–61, reflected verbatim in the National Archives note on the Berkeley Castle muniments, at *https://discovery. nationalarchives.gov.uk/details/r/56afcb9d-a2e3-4973-b8b1-aee1eca4ab0e* (accessed 18 September 2020).

5

Continuity and New Directions:
The Career of Sir Philip Clanvowe

A very different course from that followed by Master Rees and his son Philip was taken by another branch of the family. The son of William ap Hywel, and the heir to Philip ap Hywel, was Philip, who was to be known, from the earliest part of his career which can be traced, as Philip de Clanvowe. As in the case of the designation of Philip ap Rees as Philip de Bronllys, it is possible that this frenchified form was a way of obscuring his parentage, for Philip, as a son of a cleric, was illegitimate.

It is quite likely that Philip was born in the later part of the thirteenth century, probably in the years around 1290. The origin of the name de Clanvowe is contentious, and there is no clear explanation. It certainly had the effect of distancing him from the bulk of the Welsh population, amongst whom the traditional system of patronymics was still predominant. Suggestions include the notion that Clanvowe represents Cilonw near Hay, or an anglicising corruption of a place-name such as Llanfair. There are good grounds for rejecting both.[1] Instead it seems probable that the name was derived from, and identical with, that of a manor which was in the possession of Philip Clanvowe in 1340. It is also uncertain who first used the name. The record evidence suggests that Philip was the first male in the family to adopt the designation de Clanvowe, but it has also been claimed, on very tenuous evidence, that a sister of Hywel ap Meurig had married a Peter de Clavinhogh before 1290 and had brought the name into the family.[2] Again that begs the question as to why Philip, son of William ap Hywel had taken the name. The genealogies are of no help, being chaotic in their depiction of the use of the de Clanvowe name.[3] Philip's name is thus something of a mystery. But there can be no mystery about his career, which was as impressive as those of his uncles Philip ap Hywel and Master Rees ap Hywel.

The first glimpse which the records give us of Philip de Clanvowe shows that he had been involved in the movement to end the life of the king's favourite, Piers Gaveston. When Gaveston was killed on 19 June 1312 he had been cornered and captured by a group of senior barons led by the earls of Warwick, Lancaster, Arundel and Hereford. The actual killing of Gaveston was accomplished by two Welshmen, 'one of whom ran him through and the other cut off his head.'[4] It is clear that Philip de Clanvowe was in the following of the earl of Hereford, and it is probable that he had been in de Bohun's entourage when Gaveston was killed, for Philip de 'Clannon' had to be pardoned for that death in 1313.[5]

In a second major crisis of Edward II's reign Philip de Clanvowe had at least been suspected of support for the baronial opposition to the king and the Despensers, who, in the persons of Hugh the elder and his son Hugh the younger, were the particular favourites of the king. In August of 1321 Philip was pardoned for his actions against the Despensers on the testimony of – to be interpreted in this period of baronial triumph as 'at the insistence of' – the earl of Hereford, Humphrey de Bohun.[6] So Philip de Clanvowe was maintaining the family tradition of support for the earls of Hereford. A similar suspicion had been raised against Philip ap Hywel ap Meurig, and something more than suspicion had sent Master Rees to royal prisons for several years. In the case of Philip de Clanvowe, it seems that although orders were issued for his arrest in February of 1322,[7] he had managed to dispel doubts about his loyalty to the king. Immediately after the battle of Boroughbridge, a signal victory for the king, and the death or execution of the baronial leaders, orders were issued to the sheriff of Herefordshire to restore to Philip as to a number of others, their lands, goods and chattels, while the keeper of the lordships of Hay and Huntington was also ordered to return his lands and possessions to him.[8] By November of the same year, Philip de Clanvowe was so far in favour that he represented Herefordshire in the parliament.[9] Interestingly he was still standing surety for the loyalty of Herefordshire men suspected of being potential rebels.[10] Meanwhile Philip's wealth is hinted at when he lent two hundred pounds to Sir John Murdak, a Staffordshire knight.[11] It seems likely that Philip was tempted into the ranks of the victors of Boroughbridge in the period after 1322, for he is linked to the earl of Arundel, who in turn was close to the regime of the Despensers.[12]

It is, however, noticeable that Philip de Clanvowe is very quiet in the records of the mid-1320s, perhaps suggesting that his support for the Despenser-dominated regime of those years was less than wholehearted. But once a measure of stability had been restored after the turbulence of the reign of Edward II and the period of Roger Mortimer's dominance in the years before his execution in 1330, Philip de Clanvowe began his career of service to the crown and gathered a remarkable succession of offices. Many of these were in Wales and the March. Thus, in October 1331 he was deputising for the Justice of South Wales and holding an inquisition into the administration of justice throughout the southern principality.[13] In August 1332 he was appointed to array thirty men from South Wales to accompany the king to Ireland.[14] A group of three officials had already been given the task of arraying four hundred foot soldiers from South Wales, so Philip's role was a minor one. It appears that the extra troops were something of an afterthought by the king to make up numbers.

The year 1334 saw Philip again deputising for the Justice of South Wales in holding an enquiry into lands and rents granted by the bishop of St Davids to the master and chaplains of the hospital of St David, Swansea, and also presiding over an enquiry into homicides in Is Cennen and subsequent disturbances throughout much of south Wales.[15] By November he had returned to military arrangements. Specifically noted as the deputy to the Justice of South Wales he was associated with Peter Corbet, lord of Caus, and Walter de Hepton, in raising twenty men at arms and two hundred foot soldiers from South Wales and taking them to the king, who was then at Newcastle.[16] In a time of war with the Scots in the following year, Philip de Clanvowe and Owain of Montgomery, another ambitious man active in royal service, were assigned to keep the ports and coasts of south Wales, to arrest suspicious ships in those ports, and to raise men to take ships of

the Scots which were attempting to invade England.[17] Shortly afterwards the chamberlain of South Wales was ordered to provide Philip
with five hundred marks at once.[18] The next year the custody of the
south Wales ports was transferred to Rhys ap Gruffudd and Philip
de Clanvowe.[19] It seems that Rhys was now the senior official as his
name came first in the commission, but the fact that Philip was associated with such a highly regarded figure in royal administration is proof
of both his competence and the regard in which he was held by the
royal government.

The primacy of Sir Rhys ap Gruffudd in the commission for keeping
the ports in South Wales may also have been an acknowledgement that
Philip de Clanvowe had urgent business elsewhere, for at some point
in 1335 he was assigned to head an enquiry into complaints relating
to the castle and land of Builth.[20] Once more a member of the family
sprung from Hywel ap Meurig was in a position of authority in Builth,
which had played such a large part in their careers. Investigation of the
state of Builth castle led on, it seems, to a wider brief in the following year when Philip was associated with Roger Pychard and Robert
Clement in a commission to report on repairs needed in the castles
of Bwlchydinas, Newcastle Emlyn, and Blaenllyfni.[21] In 1339 Philip
returned to Builth, at the head of a commission which included Adam
Lucas, his companion in that region in 1335, and Meurig ap Rhys, to
investigate reported defects in the castle.[22] The same year was marked
by Philip's appointment to a commission, which once again included
Adam Lucas, to enquire into whether the lands, forests and chases of
Bwlchydinas, and Blaenllyfni should be regarded as appurtenant to
the castles, which had been granted to Gilbert Talbot for life without
rendering anything for them.[23] The previous custodian of the castles,
Hugh Tyrel, had handed them over to Gilbert, but had then been
informed that the treasurer and the barons of the Exchequer were
planning to continue to call him to account for the issues of the lands,
forests and chases. He appealed to the king, who set up the commission of enquiry. The commission reported that the lands and forests
and chases were indeed appurtenant to the castles, and so Hugh Tyrel
should not be burdened with payments. Philip had already begun an
inquiry into the possessions of Rhys ap Gruffudd in Lampeter, and
later in 1339 he was to be found raising a force of six hundred foot

soldiers for an expedition to Flanders.[24] These tasks were not the last that Sir Philip Clanvowe performed in Wales at this period. He was responsible for payments to Welsh troops as part of the Scottish campaign of 1341.[25]

Further assignments in Wales came in 1346–7. A particularly interesting and delicate case arose in mid-1346. The king's son, Edward the Black Prince, had ordered the arrest of a ship from Zeeland which had been stolen at sea and brought to the Cornish port of Fowey. Though arrested there, the thieves slipped away with the ship, which sailed to Haverford. The theft of the ship had caused problems in Flanders, for it had been laden with Flemish goods. Because it seemed that the English government was not trying to return the ship and its goods, the prince's wool had been seized in Flanders as retaliation. The prince had sent one of his men to secure the release of the ship from Haverford, but he had been abused by the townsfolk and driven out as had others of the prince's men. Haverford was currently in the hands of Queen Isabel, but it was supposed to revert to the prince on her death and so the prince, enraged, intervened to order the townsfolk to hand over the ship to Sir Philip de Clanvowe. So Philip had been brought in to solve a hazardous business.[26]

In November of 1346 Sir Philip, designated as the Justice of South Wales's lieutenant, was ordered to find persons of sufficient means to take over the 'farm' – that is, the renting – of Llanbadarn (Fawr) in Ceredigion, and if that should not be possible, to leave it in the hands of the present farmers. He was also ordered to keep the men whom he had arrayed in readiness until the prince should require them.[27] By February of 1347 Sir Philip appears to have solved the problem of the farm of Llanbadarn, as he had certified that the burgesses of that town wished to take over the farm for three years, answering to the prince as they had hitherto done.[28]

A more substantial problem had arisen in the course of 1347. The Justice of South Wales, Sir Thomas de Bradestan, was absent on the king's service abroad, and in his absence the usual judicial sessions had not been held. The result was the 'many extortions, damages, injuries, felonies, misprisions and other trespasses have been done in the principality of South Wales'. Sir Philip and others were ordered on 8 August to hold the sessions in the bishopric of St Davids and to give notice that they would do so. But on 17 August Sir Philip, as lieutenant of the justice Sir Thomas du Chastel Goodrich, chamberlain of South Wales, was ordered to postpone the sessions that had been arranged, as Sir Thomas de Bradestan, before whom the sessions would be held most profitably for the prince, would be returning.[29]

What is striking about Sir Philip de Clanvowe's service in Wales is the wide variety of tasks, some judicial, some military, some financial, that had fallen to him, as well as the generally high level in the administration of the southern principality and the March at which he had functioned. But there is something else which is noteworthy: his activities in Wales seem to have been few between late 1339 and 1346, with a significant gap between late 1341 and 1346. At least one reason for this pattern of involvement and apparent absence is of great significance in the story of the Clanvowes.

We have already seen that in the early 1320s Philip was involved in the politics and affairs of Herefordshire. That involvement deepened at a later stage of his career. He represented the city of Hereford in the parliament of 1337, and the county in those of 1339 and 1340.[30] But parliamentary activity was complemented by participation in the administration of Herefordshire. Thus in 1338 he was one of a group of four men, including his frequent associate Adam Lucas, appointed to a commission to array the men of Herefordshire for the defence of the realm against the French.[31] In 1340 he was included in a five-man team, led by the abbot of Wigmore, and supervised by Gilbert Talbot and the bishop of Hereford, to act as sellers of the proceeds in kind of a tax of one-ninth of goods in Herefordshire.[32] In the following year the four lay members of the group of sellers, together with the prior of Hereford, were reappointed as sellers of a ninth.[33] A group of four laymen, which included Philip de Clanvowe and two of his associates from 1340 and 1341, was appointed in 1344 to the commission of the peace for Herefordshire, a peace-keeping institution replicated all over England.[34] In October of that year Philip was one of two men who received a commission to levy in the county of Herefordshire the first year's payment of a fifteenth and tenth of the value of moveable goods for two years, which had been granted in parliament.[35] The authority of the collectors of the tax was formidable, and their presence in the county was sure to be a matter of apprehension. They were to go in person from place to place and summon two men and the reeve from each town, and the mayor and bailiffs and four good and discreet men from each city and borough, enjoining on them to cause the money to be levied by one or two of each town, city and borough and delivered to them ...

The proceeds were to be kept in the cathedral church of Hereford for safe keeping.

A similarly impressive and indeed formidable role in the county was undertaken by Sir Philip in February of 1347. He was one of four commissioners of the peace appointed for Herefordshire, to make inquisitions into 'vagabonds and those who form unlawful assemblies or otherwise disturb the peace and arrest and imprison them, certifying into the chancery the names of any who flee the county and cannot therefore be brought to justice by them, and of those arrested'.[36]

It seems that Sir Philip's significant involvement in Herefordshire coincides to a marked degree with his apparent absence from duties in Wales. This may be mere coincidence, but it does seem to represent a change of focus. It is possible that the rewards of Welsh administration were regarded by him as inadequate. In 1339 he was certainly showing concern that a fee for discharging the hereditary office of reeve in the Mortimer manor of Gladestry had not been paid for some time, and an inquisition found that it had been withheld during the whole time when Hugh Tyrel was custodian of Radnor, of which Gladestry was a part.[37] And in July of 1340 Philip acknowledged that he owed Sir Ralph Lingeyn, a significant tenant of the Mortimers of Wigmore, £220 to be levied in default of payment on Philip's lands and chattels in Herefordshire.[38] There may, however, be more fundamental reasons for a move to a much greater involvement in the affairs and administration of Herefordshire.[39]

As the heir of Philip ap Hywel Sir Philip held the house of Hergest, which was to remain in the family until the fifteenth century. His holdings both in the March and in Herefordshire were considerable. A royal charter of 1336 granted him and his heirs free warren in his demesne lands of Ocle Pychard, King's Pyon and Yazor in Herefordshire, and in Hergest, Michaelchurch by Huntington, Cusop, *Dolsuleyn* and

Llywenny in the March.[40] Several of these lands had been inherited from Philip ap Hywel.[41] He was evidently married, but his wife's identity poses a problem. A Welsh genealogy indicates that he married a daughter of Walter 'Bredwarden'.[42] But elsewhere an alternative marriage is suggested, to Philippa, a sister of Sir Richard Talbot, and daughter of the Gilbert Talbot for whom Philip acted as deputy justice of South Wales. It can certainly be established that in 1318 his wife's name was Philippa.[43] It may be that Philip was married twice, or even three times.[44] It is possible that an increasing integration into the ranks of county gentry in England may have put some strain on Sir Philip's resources, in spite of his significant landholdings[45] He seems to have died in the late 1340s. It is possible that he may have been a plague victim, but this is no more than a conjecture.

Whatever its causes, the apparent switch of Philip de Clanvowe's focus from Welsh to Herefordshire administration was unprecedented in his family in terms of scale. It marked the increasing detachment of his family from Welsh affairs, and an increasing involvement in Herefordshire, which was to form the basis for a growing closeness to the royal court. It is also clear, as far as we can tell from the available evidence, that although Sir Philip was frequently involved in the administration of Wales and the Welsh March, and although such involvement brought him into association with important members of the Welsh ministerial aristocracy, the majority of his associates were English, and that amongst them men like Adam Lucas had a particular connection with Herefordshire.[46] Though the grandson of Hywel ap Meurig, Philip de Clanvowe was beginning to resemble the English administrator in Wales. His base was no longer firmly in the March, but in Herefordshire, where he had acquired several properties, including Yazor, which was to become the mausoleum of the Clanvowe dynasty, and other manors located in a chain extending to the eastern parts of the county.[47] Here was a first step in the family's eventual turn away from Wales to other fields of interest.

Notes

[1]   Richard Morgan, 'An extent of the lordship of Hay', *Brycheiniog*, 28 (1995–96), 15–21, at p. 20, has an excellent discussion.

2   See, for example, M. C. Seymour, 'Sir John Clanvowe, 1341–91', *Transactions of the Radnorshire Society*, 75 (2005), 35–58, at p. 35, following the (tentative and highly suspect) genealogy in Bartrum, *Welsh Genealogies*, 4, Rhys ap Tewdwr 26.

3   See previous note.

4   Haines, *King Edward II*, p. 86; N. Denholm-Young (ed.), *Vita Edwardi Secundi* (London, 1957), p. 27: *traditus est Walensibus duobus, de quibus transfodit hic corpus, amputavit ille caput.*

5   *Calendar of Patent Rolls, 1313–17*, p. 23; 'Clannon' is to be read as a rendering of 'Clanvou'.

6   *Calendar of Patent Rolls, 1321–24*, p. 18

7   Ibid., p. 77.

8   *Calendar of Close Rolls, 1318–23*, pp. 430, 433.

9   Griffiths, *Principality of Wales*, p. 103.

10 *Calendar of Fine Rolls, 1319–27*, p. 172, where Philip de Clanvowe stands surety for Geoffrey de Beaufour, along with John Charlton, lord of Powys, Robert de Sapy, Thomas le Blunt of co. Gloucester, Simon de Kinardesle and Richard de Penebrugg of co. Hereford, who together pledge 200 marks. Ibid., p. 234, where William Waldeboef finds sureties for £40: these were Hugh de Mortimer, Roger Pychard, Emery Pauncefoot knights, and Philip Clanvowe. The other sureties were all major figures in the March, and Philip's association with them is a clue to his status even at this early stage in his career.

11 *Calendar of Close Rolls, 1323–27*, p. 166.

12 Arundel himself appears to have been building bridges to former adversaries in the years after 1322. Notable in the present context was his success in arranging a marriage between his daughter Alice and John de Bohun, the heir to Humphrey, earl of Hereford and Essex, in May 1325. See Michael Burtscher, *The FitzAlans, Earls of Arundel and Surrey, Lords of the Welsh Marches (1267–1415)* (Almeley: Logaston Press, 2008), p. 21.

13 *Calendar of Inquisitions, Miscellaneous*, II, pp. 321–2.

14 *Calendar of Patent Rolls, 1330–34*, p. 321.

15 *Calendar of Patent Rolls, 1334–8*, p. 20; *Calendar of Inquisitions, Miscellaneous*, II, p. 346.

16 *Rotuli Scottie*, I, pp. 289, 314.

17 Ibid., p. 365. For a survey of the career of Owen de Montgomery, see John Davies, 'Owen of Montgomery: Priest, King's Clerk and Military Officer', *Montgomeryshire Collections*, 104 (2016), pp. 17–24.

18 Ibid., p. 367.

19 Ibid., p. 427.

20 *Calendar of Inquisitions, Miscellaneous*, II, p. 350.

21 *Calendar of Inquisitions, Miscellaneous*, II, p. 364.

22 *Calendar of Patent Rolls, 1338–40*, p. 284.
23 *Calendar of Close Rolls, 1339–41*, pp. 316–17.
24 *Calendar of Patent Rolls, 1338–40*, p. 279. TNA, SC6/1221/3 m. 8;/4 m. 4.
25 TNA, SC6/1221/3 no. 2 m. 1.
26 *Register of Edward the Black Prince Part I A.D. 1346–1348* (London: HMSO, 1930), pp. 4–5.
27 Ibid., p. 32.
28 Ibid., p. 45.
29 Ibid., pp. 108, 113.
30 Griffiths, *Principality of Wales*, p. 103.
31 *Calendar of Patent Rolls, 1338–40*, p. 135.
32 Ibid., p. 502.
33 *Calendar of Patent Rolls, 1340–43*, p. 155.
34 *Calendar of Patent Rolls, 1343–45*, p. 395.
35 *Calendar of Fine Rolls, 1337–47*, p. 391.
36 *Calendar of Patent Rolls, 1345–48*, p. 301.
37 *Calendar of Inquisitions, Miscellaneous*, II, p. 404 (no. 1643).
38 *Calendar of Close Rolls, 1339–41*, p. 490.
39 See below, pp. 114–15, 119.
40 *Calendar of Charter Rolls, 1327–41*, p. 352. The lands noted here do not amount to the whole of Philip's interests. See below, p. 112.
41 See *Inquisitions and Assessments relating to Feudal Aids*, vol. 2, p. 394, for Philip de Clanvowe's tenure of a knight's fee in Ocle Pychard *quod Philippus ap Howel nuper tenuit*.
42 *Welsh Genealogies*, p. 801, sub Rhys ap Tewdwr 26. This alleged wife was obviously a member of the de Bredwardine family of Bredwardine, Herefordshire.
43 See M. C. Seymour, 'Sir John Clanvowe 1341–1391', *Transactions of the Radnorshire Society*, 75 (2005), 35–58, at p. 36: Seymour cites in support of this K. B. McFarlane, *Lancastrian Kings and Lollard Knights* (Oxford: The Clarendon Press, 1972), p. 230. There (at p. 231) we find that 'from *Calendar of Papal Petitions 1342–1419*, ed. W. H. Bliss (1896) i. 261, we learn that he [John, Philip's son and heir] was nephew of Sir Richard Talbot of Mar (c.1305–56), whose widow married Sir John Bromwich …; it looks as if Philip Clanvow married Richard Talbot's sister. This is supported by the fact that Philip Clanvow was deputy to Gilbert Talbot, Richard's father, as Justice of South Wales on 24 September 1344 (*Cal. Pat. Rolls, 1334–8*, p. 20.)' It will be evident that McFarlane's date of 24 September 1344 is an error for the same day in 1334.
44 See pp. 76 and 113.
45 See Seymour, 'Sir John Clanvowe' p. 36, and McFarlane, *Lancastrian Kings and Lollard Knights*', p. 230; also p. 75 and notes 37–8.

[46] See the fine of 1328 (TNA CP 25/1/82/37, no. 7) by which Adam Lucas and his wife Cecily succeeded in a plea of covenant against the alleged deforciant relating to lands in Brinsop and Burghill, so that 'Hugh (the deforciant) has granted to Adam and Cecily the tenements and has rendered them to them in the court, to hold to Adam and Cecily and the heirs of Adam, of the chief lords for ever'. For Adam Lucas's involvement with Philip de Clanvowe, see the following: the Commission of 1335 to Philip de Clanvowe and Adam Lucas to enquire into complaints regarding the castle and land of Builth (*Calendar of Inquisitions, Miscellaneous*, p. 350); the Commission of 1338 to named men to array the men of the county of Hereford for the defence of the realm against the French, to keep the peace there and to hear and determine trespasses: Peter de Grandison, Roger Chandos, Richard de Pembrigg, Philip de Clanvowe, Adam Lucas (*Calendar of Patent Rolls, 1338–40*, p. 135); the Commission to Philip de Clanvowe, Adam Lucas and Meurig ap Rees to make inquisition regarding reported defects in Builth castle (ibid., p. 284); and the appointment of Peter de Grandison, Philip de Clanvowe, Adam Lucas and John de Mershton to enquire as to the issues of lands, forests and chases appurtenant to the castles of Bwlchydinas and Blaenllyfni with the result that a former keeper, Hugh Tyrel should not be charged with those issues (*Calendar of Close Rolls, 1339–41*, pp. 316–17).

[47] For further analysis, see p. 114 and the map at p. xvii.

6

The Last of the Line:
The Later Clanvowes

By the mid-fourteenth century the members of the Clanvowe family were moving increasingly into a world far removed from the Welsh March. They became a prominent force in the governance of Herefordshire and their territorial base remained in that county, but the focus of their careers was increasingly directed towards the royal court. Thus John Clanvowe, son of Philip de Clanvowe represented Herefordshire in the parliament of January 1348 and was a squire in the household of Edward III in the following year.[1] In 1354 John and his wife Matilda were given a papal indult (licence) to choose their own confessors who would give them plenary remission at the hour of their death.[2] Such a grant of papal indulgence was not made without a significant payment. It is possible that at this point they were both elderly, though having lived through the period of the Black Death it is possible that they were concerned to make arrangements in anticipation of a second visitation. In the same year a further sign of fragility, as also perhaps of past distinguished service, came with a royal exemption for life for John de Clanvowe from being put against his will on assizes, juries or recognitions and from appointment as mayor, sheriff, escheator, coroner or other minister of the king.[3] A further indication of John's status and perhaps of the size of his purse is provided by the grant of market and fair rights in Michaelchurch (on Arrow) in January 1354. John was to have a weekly market, and fairs at Michaelmas and on the octave of (the eighth day after) Holy Trinity.[4] The revenue from such grants might be significant, though markedly uncertain in an age dominated by plague; even so they almost automatically placed the recipients in the ranks of the higher gentry and the baronage.

John de Clanvowe appears to have died by 1361.[5] His younger brother Thomas had served as sheriff of Herefordshire in 1348.[6] These offices and the clear signs of royal favour suggest well-regarded men who were amongst the mainstays of administration in the fourteenth century, sometimes in very difficult circumstances. But they still do not compare with the career of the most interesting of the later Clanvowes, Sir John, whose immediate ancestry is somewhat mysterious. It is uncertain whether he was a son of John or of Thomas. The former is perhaps more likely, and it is clear that he was John's heir.[7]

This younger John came of age in 1362, succeeding to a significant scatter of lands in Herefordshire and the March.[8] That old connections were still important is demonstrated by the fact in the early part of his career he was first squire and then knight in the household of Humphrey de Bohun, seventh earl of Hereford (also sixth earl of Essex and second earl of Northampton).[9] After Earl Humphrey's death in 1373, and the failure of the de Bohun dynasty in the male line, Sir John went into royal service, as a knight in the households first of Edward III and then of Richard II. Already he had been active as a soldier in royal armies, serving in France in 1364, possibly in an expedition to Castile in 1366, and then from 1369 onwards he was frequently active in military service in France and subsequently in Spain.[10] Such service brought substantial rewards. As a knight in the household of Humphrey de Bohun he had received an annuity of £40; his annuity was continued when he passed from Earl Humphrey's service, following the latter's death, to that of Edward III in 1373 and was augmented by a further grant of £50 per year.[11] In 1381 this second annuity was further increased to one hundred marks, and he was granted the stewardship of Haverford castle for life.[12] A further grant gave him the custody of the forest of Snowdon, and a reversionary interest in that of Merioneth.[13] In 1385 he exchanged his annuities of £50 and one hundred marks for all the revenues of the town, castle and lordship of Haverford, again for life.[14] This source of income was further augmented in 1388 with the grant of the prisage of wines – a royal tax of two tuns of wine from every ship importing twenty tuns or more – at Haverford.[15] He thus had significant financial interests in north Wales and in the southern March.

Those interests of course might entail responsibilities; thus in April of 1383 he was associated with another Herefordshire man, Sir Simon Burley, in a commission of Oyer et Terminer 'touching divers offences in the king's lordship of Haverford in Wales'.[16] A broader remit had been signalled by an order of 21 May 1381. Clanvowe (second on the list, and noted as a knight of the chamber) was appointed, with Hugh de Segrave (Steward of the Household, heading the list), David Cradock, Justice of Wales, David Hanmer, serjeant at law, Hugh Young and John Woodhouse, chamberlains of south and north Wales, to survey the condition of Wales and its people, and those of the lordship of Haverford, and to talk with certain of them and take order for the general peace, and explain and declare to them certain matters affecting the condition of the realm and of Wales and the king, and after colloquy and agreement with the people of those parts report and certify to the king what passes between them. A further order to them, issued on the following day, empowered the group to grant, as they should think expedient, pardons in the king's name to any persons for trespasses against the peace, misprisions, extorsions, etc., in cases not pending before the king's justices.[17] The government was clearly very concerned about the state of Wales. The orders were issued just over a week before the outbreak of the Peasants' Revolt, but the government was apparently looking in the wrong direction, for that rising began in Essex and spread through much of eastern England. But it has to be considered, and it can only be a conjecture, whether the pacifying activities of Segrave, Clanvowe and their colleagues may have helped to keep the insurgency out of Wales. Clanvowe's involvement in Wales cannot have lasted for long, as he was quickly assigned the task of joining the mission led by Sir Simon Burley to Prague, to arrange the marriage of Richard II with Anne of Bohemia, the sister of Wenzel, king of the Romans.[18]

A further intriguing appointment came in May of 1385, when it was recorded that John Clanvowe, knight of the chamber, was

> about to proceed to South and West Wales with special mandate to act on behalf of the king in examining the conditions of those parts and doing all that is necessary for the peace and good government of the same, with power to lodge himself and his people within the king's fortalices

[fortified places or houses] there and to compel all the king's bailiffs and ministers to furnish victuals, carriages, and messengers, when required, at reasonable prices, and with power to grant security to all persons outlawed who come in, and to arrest and do justice on all rebels, the king undertaking to ratify his proceedings herein.[19]

In effect, Clanvowe had been given a free hand in dealing with the governance of the southern principality.

The scope of the powers granted to Sir John is impressive and testifies to his trusted position as a royal knight. So does the apparent nature of at least one of the problems which he had been appointed to solve. The tenor of his appointment suggests serious disorder in the southern principality and an onerous task awaiting Clanvowe. It is likely that the problem related to the highest levels of governance in the southern principality, for there is evidence of a serious break-down of order there. John Lawrence, a burgess of Carmarthen, sheriff of the county, and deputy to the Justice of South Wales had had to be pardoned on two occasions in May 1384 and February 1385 for all felonies for which he had been indicted, the only exceptions being rapes, murders and treason. The Justice, Nicholas Audley, who had been Justiciar in 1382 and was appointed for life in February 1385 seems to have had just as violent a reputation, being accused of a formidable array of offences over the course of his Justiciarship, including some complicity in the murder of John Lawrence in October of 1385.[20] This appears to have been Clanvowe's last significant assignment in Wales, coming at the close of a five-year period in which he had been given a succession of missions in the principality.

But in the event Sir John's task in Wales was once again over quickly – perhaps all too quickly in view of the Lawrence murder a few months later. By July he was back in England and involved in an invasion of Scotland. In August he was associated with his friend Sir William Neville and the latter's brother, Alexander, archbishop of York, to inspect all castles and fortifications both royal and others in the March of Scotland and to organise the men of the region, including those of great magnates such as Henry Percy and John de Neville, to defend the Scottish March. It was to be amongst his last military expeditions on behalf of the king, though in September 1386 he was associated once more with Sir William Neville to visit Orwell on the Suffolk coast to check on its readiness to face a possible French attack, and he took a small party of troops to reinforce the garrison at Calais in November of the same year.

In fact, as a man with wide experience of many aspects of governance, and one clearly trusted by the king, Sir John was almost inevitably drawn into the world of diplomacy. As early as 1378 he had been a guest of Duke John IV of Brittany, who was living in England in exile.[21] He his membership of the embassy of Sir Simon Burley to Prague in 1381 has already been noticed.[22] From 1386 onwards his diplomatic duties were frequent, involving in that year and subsequent years discussions with the French on extending a truce and a mission to Portugal to conclude an alliance.[23] In June 1389 he was a member of an embassy which agreed a truce with France at Leulingham between Calais and Boulogne. In 1389 he was also involved in negotiations with Duke John of Brittany at Calais in August, and in November he was sent to report on the keeping of the port of Brest, which had an English garrison.[24]

The following year saw Clanvowe joining a group led by the earl of Devon, which also included once more Sir William Neville, to participate in a French crusade against the emir of Tunis.[25] The combined force left Genoa in June 1390, and after somewhat inconclusive fighting returned by October. Once back in England he was appointed in November to an embassy to Flanders, while early in 1391 he was involved in diplomatic activity in advance of a projected meeting between King Richard and Charles VI of France.[26] This was his last diplomatic mission, for later in the year he and Sir William Neville set off overseas. The object of their journey is unknown. It is possible that they had decided to offer help to the Byzantine emperor, Manuel II for an embassy from the emperor, seeking western help, had apparently been in Genoa in 1390. Whatever its object the journey was to prove fatal to both men. They died in or near to Constantinople in October 1391. The suggestion is that they were victims of plague. Plague seems generally to have killed those affected within a very few days so it is possible that Clanvowe and Neville may have contracted it from travellers who had picked it up rather earlier. It is known that there was an outbreak of plague at this time in the Morea which lay on the final stage of their journey, and may have been the ultimate source of later waves of infections.[27] They were buried in a joint tomb, discovered in a mosque in the city in 1913. The tomb slab showed their helms facing each other as though kissing, and their shields overlapping. On the shields their coats of arms had been impaled – that is, each shield showed half of the coat of arms of each man, a device usually reserved for depiction of the arms of a husband and a wife. The appearance is of a close relationship between Clanvowe and Neville.[28]

The frequency of Sir John's military and diplomatic engagements is impressive. But they by no means exhaust the scope of his commitments. In the midst of official assignments he had apparently found time for involvement in London literary circles. A friendship with Chaucer is strongly suggested by Sir John's involvement in a potential scandal concerning the great poet in the Spring of 1381. On 1 May, Sir John Clanvowe, Sir William Neville, Sir William Beauchamp, and two London aldermen, John Philpot and Richard Morel, witnessed a statutory declaration by Cecily Chaumpaigne absolving Chaucer of all charges and actions of rape against her. It seems that Chaucer had been the victim of false accusations and had asked some of his prominent friends to support him in countering them.[29] Sir John was himself something of a literary figure. The idea that he was the author of the poem *The Cuckoo and the Nightingale*, or *The Book of Cupid* has given rise to controversy.[30] For centuries regarded as the work of Geoffrey Chaucer himself, by the twentieth century opinion about the poem was changing. W. W. Skeet suggested that the poem was the work of a Clanvowe, and opted for Sir Thomas (d. 1410) as the author.[31] G. L. Kittredge, professor of English Literature at Harvard, writing in 1903, agreed that 'there is no reason to doubt that Clanvowe was the author's name',[32] but argued that the poem should be attributed not to Sir Thomas, but to Sir John Clanvowe, whom he calls 'Chaucer's poetical disciple'.[33] Both Skeat and Kittredge noted that in one of the manuscripts in which the poem is preserved the text is followed by the words 'Explicit Clanvowe' (Clanvowe has finished). This they took as an attribution of authorship. There remained, however, room for scepticism of the Clanvowe attribution. In 1961 Dr Ethel Seaton maintained that the author of *The Book of Cupid* was the fifteenth-century courtier and poet Sir Richard Roos, an attribution which has won little support.[34] In a paper published in 1984,[35] William McColly of the University of South Carolina applied a statistical approach to the poem's text, focusing on the use of 'function words'. These were described as 'prepositions, conjunctions, auxiliaries, articles, and certain adverbs, pronouns and adjectives, these function-words are assumed to have a somewhat constant rate of occurrence from work to work of the same genre and type of the same author, but to vary from author to author'.[36] On the basis of this somewhat dubious framework, supplemented by some more conventional stylistic analysis, McColly concluded that *The Book of Cupid* was assuredly not the work of Chaucer though he added that 'no brief is held for Clanvowe as the author of *The Book of Cupid*'.[37] But in a splendid introduction to, and edition of, the poem, Danna Symons of the University of Rochester, New York State, began her analysis with the comment that 'With *The Boke of Cupide, God of Love* John Clanvowe begins a modern English literary tradition.' The accompanying note introduces a further influential name to the debate and states that 'Although other possibilities have been put forward, Sir John Clanvowe is the most likely author of the poem. See V. J. Scattergood, "The Authorship of *The Boke of Cupide*." Scattergood also includes a brief discussion in his introduction to *The Works of Sir John Clanvowe*, pp. 22–25.'[38]

And yet some modern critics have shown a similar agnosticism to that of McColly regarding a Clanvowe authorship. As has been noted above, this is the case with the Chaucer scholar M. C. Seymour, who has argued that the 'Explicit Clanvowe' statement – in a hand of *c.*1450 – should not be accepted uncritically as an indication of authorship. He explains that it may just as well 'denote scribe (Sir John or Thomas writing out a composition by another for a friend's collection, like the explicit on f. 67^v of the same manuscript); it may simply be a misattribution'.[39] Seymour adds in relation to Sir John that 'a connection between this busy and sober Lollard knight and this light-hearted and skilfully composed love poem written for a celebration of St Valentine's Day at court is … extremely doubtful.'[40]

But we should note that, *pace* Seymour, it is hardly reasonable to deny Sir John Clanvowe's authorship of *The Book of Cupid* on the grounds that it is stylistically different from the tract *The Two Ways*, which is acknowledged to have been written by Sir John. *The Two*

Ways and *The Book of Cupid* were written at different times and in very different circumstances; also, one is a poem in, it would seem, conscious imitation of Chaucer, while the other is a prose devotional tract written very close to the end of Sir John Clanvowe's life and therefore much more likely to strike a serious and devotional note. As we shall see, it is by no means certain that Sir John was a Lollard, and it simply does not follow that even if he adopted a serious and sober attitude towards spiritual matters, he was incapable of the sort of light-hearted celebration of St Valentine's day that we find in *The Book of Cupid*. Sir John Clanvowe was a household knight in the court of Richard II, and it is not at all unlikely that the construction of such *jeux d'esprit* were regular occurrences amongst the knights of the chamber. We should also remember that Chaucer himself was quite capable of imparting very different moods and attitudes to characters and scenarios across his different works. *The Book of Cupid* was almost certainly composed for performance in the presence of Richard II's queen, and if the queen in question was, as seems likely, Anne of Bohemia, we should recall that Sir John had a close relationship with her, as he was one of the envoys sent to Prague to arrange her marriage to Richard and that he had been one of her escorts on the journey to England, as well as being present at her wedding in January 1382. This is not to say that authorship by Sir Thomas should be lightly ruled out: he too was a knight of the royal household, and his wife Perryne had been one of Anne of Bohemia's ladies in waiting. Both Sir John and Sir Thomas therefore had significant contacts with the queen. Sir Thomas still has his supporters as the author of *The Book of Cupid*, but the weight of circumstance and of scholarly opinion seems to incline more towards Sir John.

But Sir John is known to have been an author, albeit of more sombre literature. Late in his life he produced a treatise, *The Two Ways*, the manuscript of which survives in University College, Oxford, which was an exhortation to virtue.[41] Its ten thousand words consist mainly of conventional piety, but it contains one very interesting section in which reference is made to:

> Such folk as would prefer to live meekly in this world and refrain from riot, noise and strife, and live simply and eat and drink in moderation

and clothe themselves modestly, and suffer patiently wrongs that other
folk do and say to them ... and desire no great fame or reward ... such
folk the world scorns and calls them *lolleris*, worthless, fools and shame-
ful wretches ...

The word *lolleris* is close to, and related to, Lollards, the alleged followers of Wycliffe, who were coming under attack in the later
fourteenth century as being heretics. The passage quoted, suggesting
that Clanvowe himself was amongst those who had been labelled as
Lollards, is intriguing. It is very close to an admission of affinity to
the Lollards, if not to an acceptance of all their beliefs.[42] And indeed
Sir John Clanvowe has been counted amongst the group of household
knights of Richard II who were sympathetic to the Lollards, and in
some cases may have been converts to their doctrines.[43] There is no
sign of evident heresy in Clanvowe's work, but it is entirely possible
that he was receptive to some Lollard ideas. But if Clanvowe makes
no explicit statement that can be labelled as heretical, his silences are
more significant. He makes no reference to the spiritual apparatus
of the Church, such as pilgrimage, the sacraments, the veneration of
saints, and even the efficacy of the priesthood. There is an implication
in Clanvowe's work that the thing that concerns him is the direct relationship between man and God. And there lay one of the chief roots
of heresy. It has been well said that 'Sir John's treatise displays a strain
of deep lay piety, apparently unconnected with the Church, which is
almost a hallmark of early Lollardy.'[44]

All that can be said with certainty is that Sir John Clanvowe was
identified by the contemporary chronicler, Thomas Walsingham,
working mainly at St Albans abbey, as one of the 'Lollard knights', as
was his friend Sir William Neville, and others whom he worked with,
like Sir Lewis Clifford who led the embassy of 1390, which included
Clanvowe, to make arrangements for the meeting of the English and
French kings.[45] Clanvowe, Clifford and Sir Richard Sturry – another
knight named as a Lollard by Walsingham – had been executors in
1385–86 of the will of Joan of Kent, princess of Wales, who had been
a protector of Wycliffe.[46] It is possible therefore that Clanvowe was a
member of a group of like-minded knights whose simple piety led
them to a position not far removed from early Lollardy and caused

them to be associated with heretical beliefs. In some cases, in the years after Clanvowe's death, some of those knights came to be more attracted to Lollard beliefs, though for the most part they were careful not to parade their sympathy for the heretics.

Clanvowe faced potentially greater dangers in the tumultuous politics of Richard II's reign. As a trusted household knight, he was inevitably close to a king whose belief in the majesty of his position and his right to unfettered powers brought him into conflict with many barons and parliaments alike. In those circumstances, political crises were inevitable. One such broke in 1387–88, when a group of magnates, the Lords Appellant, joined with their supporters in the so-called Merciless Parliament, to humble the monarch by removing many of his ministers and supporters from the court. Several of Richard II's principal officials were executed, including some of the household knights. Amongst these was Sir Simon Burley, with whom Clanvowe had several times been associated.[47] Sir John was perhaps lucky to escape.

Clanvowe had not entirely lost contact with his family's roots: we have seen that for a relatively limited period, particularly in the early and mid-1380s he was periodically engaged in Welsh business, and some of the rewards of his service to the kings were grants of lands and offices in Wales. His principal property lay in Herefordshire, and he possessed the house at Hergest apparently begun by his ancestor Hywel ap Meurig.[48] Many of his lands were held of the Mortimer family, and he had been a member of the household of Humphrey de Bohun, earl of Hereford, as had so many of his family before him. It is, however, noticeable that he had not been amongst the Mortimer retainers who are listed in this period.[49] He had been a commissioner of the peace for Herefordshire.[50] But all of these facets of his life had been less significant than his position at the royal court, and his overseas service in the royal interest in both military and diplomatic contexts. These activities and interests brought him far more expansive horizons than any previous member of his family. He clearly maintained his family's trajectory into the upper ranks of English society, but now in a national as well as a regional context.

Sir John was frequently appointed to commissions which included senior members of the aristocracy as well as prominent members of the knightly class. Thus, his role as a commissioner for the peace in

Herefordshire in 1382 entailed acting with the bishop of Hereford and the earl of Buckingham. More significantly he was one of those selected to hear the case between William Montague, earl of Salisbury and John de Montague in February 1386.[51] His fellow commissioners included two bishops (of Winchester and Exeter), and three earls (of Arundel, Oxford and Nottingham), as well as Hugh Segrave, whom he already knew from a Welsh commission of 1381, by now treasurer of England, and Simon de Burley, vice-chamberlain. In October of 1386 he was also one of many deponents in the celebrated case of *Scrope v Grosvenor* regarding the right to bear specific arms. Sir John's deposition in favour of Sir Richard Scrope was characterised by Sir Harris Nicolas as being 'chiefly remarkable for the petulance which he displayed at being interrogated'. Clanvowe roundly declared that 'if one were to put all of the interrogatories in the world to him, he would answer once for all, and say, certainly, that wherever he was armed in the King's wars he never saw any man bear the said arms, nor use them, but those of the name of Scrope; and before this debate he had heard nothing of the Grosvenors or their ancestry.'[52] It may be unfair to describe this testimony as petulant, though it was perhaps a little arch, which is perhaps understandable from a witness with the ancestry of Sir John Clanvowe.

His diplomatic and other ventures maintained that sort of high-level contact with English magnates. Sir John's various assignments also consolidated his relationship with a close-knit circle of friends, most particularly Sir William Neville, but also including men such as Sir William Beauchamp, baron Abergavenny, with whom he frequently served.[53] Record sources reveal that Sir John's role as a chamber knight involved him in many varied tasks. Though Tout may have been unjust in individual cases in categorising the chamber knights of Richard II as 'an unpopular class ... loose livers, military only in name, and strangely contrasted with the distinguished soldiers who were knights of Edward III's chamber', his further judgement that 'they, with the esquires of the chamber, were ever convenient instruments to execute any king's work that came along' is more applicable to Sir John and his colleagues.[54]

That momentum into the higher reaches of English politics was largely, if not quite as fully, maintained by Sir John's successor,

Sir Thomas Clanvowe. A mystery surrounds Sir Thomas's parentage. Sir John Clanvowe is not known to have married, and no sons are recorded. It is still quite possible that Sir Thomas was a son of Sir John. It is, however, possible that Thomas was Sir John's nephew, and even that he was a younger brother. But it is tolerably clear that Thomas was Sir John's heir.

Several of Sir John Clanvowe's old associations were maintained by Sir Thomas: he worked alongside colleagues of Sir John such as John Scudamore and Walter Devereux.[55] He maintained friendship with William Beauchamp, lord Abergavenny,[56] and was clearly close to members of the group of so-called 'Lollard Knights' amongst whom Sir John had been counted. Of the group named with Sir John Clanvowe as Lollard knights by Walsingham in 1387, Sir Lewys Clifford, Sir Richard Sturry, Sir Thomas Latimer, Sir William Neville, Sir John Montague and Sir John Cheyne, several were to have close links to Sir Thomas Clanvowe. Thus, Cheyne and Latimer were involved in William Beauchamp's acquisition of Ewyas Harold,[57] while the overseers of Sir Lewys Clifford's will in 1404 were Sir Thomas Clanvowe, Sir John Cheyne and Sir Philip de la Vache, another old associate of Sir John Clanvowe.[58]

It seems that Sir Thomas was rather more rooted in the Herefordshire traditions of the family: he served as a Justice for the county between 1397 and 1399, was sheriff in the same period, and acted as M.P. for the county in 1394 and in the parliaments of January 1397 and September of that year.[59] His marriage to Perryne Whitney in 1392 cemented his interests in Herefordshire for his wife's father, Sir Robert Whitney, who was a prominent Herefordshire magnate, had represented the county in the parliaments of 1377, 1379, 1380 and 1391, as well as acting as sheriff in 1377–78.[60]

But his father-in-law also had a post at the royal court: he became a retainer of Richard II with an annuity of forty marks and the post of herberger of the household, and this may have helped Thomas in his career.[61] Certainly Thomas himself had close contacts with the royal court. He was particularly involved with the household of Richard II's queen, the (very) young Isabella, and in 1399 took New Year's gifts to her parents Charles VI and Isabel of France.[62] After the fall of Richard II, Sir Thomas appears to have accepted, and to have been accepted by, the regime of Henry IV. Richard II's grants to him and his wife were confirmed by the new king in October 1399.[63] He was amongst the party charged with the task of taking Isabella back to France in 1401.[64]

It seems likely that the readiness with which Sir Thomas Clanvowe accepted the new regime of Henry IV can in large part be explained in terms of the relationship between national and county or regional governance. As long as the new regime was prepared to accept, in all but a few cases, the existing structures of local governance, especially that exercised by burgeoning county communities, it could usually rely on local cooperation. Thomas's 'reliability' as a man prepared to accept and work with the new regime of Henry IV is demonstrated by his appointment in May 1402 as one of a small group of magnates in each county – in his case Herefordshire – whose task it was to oppose lies that were being spread to the effect that 'the king has not kept the promises he made at his advent into the realm and at his coronation and in Parliaments and councils that the laws and laudable customs of the realm should be conserved.'[65] Those appointed – and in the case of Herefordshire they numbered ten – were to

> bring to the notice of the king's lieges … that it always has been and will be the king's intention that the common wealth and laws and customs of the same realm shall be observed and kept and that the impugners of the same and the preachers of those lies and their maintainers shall be punished, to enquire about the names of all such, and to assemble the king's lieges of the county to resist them and to arrest and imprison all persons preaching such lies and to certify thereon to the king and council from time to time.

So Sir Thomas was set to become one of the stalwarts of the new regime of Henry IV, until another pressing issue diverted him.

It was just a little later in 1402 that Sir Thomas learned how hard it was to shake off his heritage in the March. He was part of the force assembled by Sir Edmund Mortimer to oppose an incursion into the Middle March by Owain Glyn Dŵr. Several of the Herefordshire gentry were present, including Sir Robert Whitney, Thomas's father-in-law, and Sir Kinard de la Bere.[66] When the opposing armies met at

Pilleth (Bryn Glas) in Maelienydd on 22 June, the outcome was disas-trous for Mortimer's force. An apparent defection by Mortimer's Welsh archers from Maelienydd left his men helpless. By the end of the battle Sir Robert Whitney and Sir Kinard de la Bere lay dead; Sir Edmund Mortimer was a captive, and so too was Sir Thomas Clanvowe. His capture is recorded in the *Annals of Owain Glyn Dŵr*, a short chroni-cle which survives only in a sixteenth-century manuscript. It is not a substantial account of the Glyn Dŵr years and in some respects is of suspect accuracy, but the fact that it mentions Sir Thomas Clanvowe by name suggests his prominence. In fact, the only two captives from the battle of Bryn Glas mentioned in the annals are Sir Edmund Mortimer and Sir Thomas Clanvowe.[67]

We have to assume that Sir Thomas was released by Glyn Dŵr upon payment of a ransom. Certainly, he had arrived in England by the start of November.[68] The date of his release may well be of signifi-cance. The other principal captives held by Glyn Dŵr were Edmund Mortimer, and Reginald de Grey, lord of Ruthin. Reginald de Grey was granted permission to raise a ransom on 13 October, and arrange-ments were made for the first instalment (of 6,000 marks) to be paid on 11 November. It is possible that the captives were held together, in which case Mortimer would have seen the release of Sir Thomas Clanvowe and would have known of the arrangements being put in place for Reginald de Grey's release. Meanwhile, nothing was being done about a ransom for Mortimer. Even if the captives were not being held together, it is unlikely that Glyn Dŵr would not have told Mortimer of the release and impending release of the others. It is thus probable that the release of the other captives was of crucial importance in determining Mortimer to abandon hope of a ransom and to throw in his lot with Glyn Dŵr. By the end of November he had married Catherine, Owain's daughter, and in mid-December he was writing to his tenantry to announce his change of sides.[69]

It is likely that some at least of Clanvowe's properties near the border suffered at the hands of Glyn Dŵr's forces, just as a significant num-ber of churches did.[70] It is almost certainly significant that Thomas's archives containing important royal letters disappeared, presumably taken by Glyn Dŵr's men or simply burned. He was subsequently issued with an exemplification (a copy) of his royal grants. He had gone into the Chancery and sworn an oath that his original letters containing royal grants had disappeared, and he did this before 1 November, thus suggesting that he had been released by Glyn Dŵr some days previously.[71] And in 1404 he was granted 'that nothing shall be taken of his goods to the king's use and none of the king's lieges shall be lodged within the mansions or possessions of himself or his poor tenants in the county of Hereford and the Marches of Wales.'[72] Not only is that grant a sign of the damage that had been inflicted upon Sir Thomas's properties, but with its mention of his lands in Herefordshire and the March it gives a hint as to the extent of his lands. At his death in 1410 his will contained an instruction that he was to be buried at the Herefordshire church of Yazor, the place of 'myn auncestres'. But the will was dated at Hergest, so the family had retained its residence there.[73]

Sir Thomas's bruising encounter with Glyn Dŵr's insurgent forces was amongst the last signs of an enduring involvement with Wales. In other ways he seems in some respects to have followed the lead of Sir John Clanvowe, nowhere more evidently than in his association with the Lollards. We have seen that there was a distinct clerical element in the sons of Hywel ap Meurig, even if they also displayed some very worldly talents and interests. With Sir John Clanvowe, and with Sir Thomas, a clear spiritual dimension reappears, but with them it seems to have taken the form of an association, however discreet – and in Sir John's case it was not always so – with those suspected of heresy. His neighbours in Herefordshire included several people who were, or were to be, associated with Lollardy. These included John Croft and the notorious Sir John Oldcastle. Thomas was more than once linked with Lollardy. Sometimes it is the silence of the records rather than any explicit connections that is potentially significant. Thus, Thomas may have been active in defending the Welsh Lollard Walter Brut in 1393, 'for it is notable that both he and his father-in-law Whitney, though resident in the March at the time, were absent from the commission set up to suppress the Welsh [L]ollard's supporters'.[74] And when he died in 1410 his will contained several elements reminiscent of Lollard attitudes. It is probably significant that no bequests were made to the church or to religious houses.[75] Similarly his will reveals an opposition to ceremony in burial and a revulsion towards the corpse of the deceased person, which seem to be characteristic of Lollards or Lollard sympathisers. When his wife Perryne died in 1422 her will was more explicit, containing references to some devotional tracts which have been regarded, on somewhat inadequate grounds, as being infected with Lollard belief.[76]

Even more important, at the time of Sir Thomas's death, his will had as one of its executors, Roger Partrich, a Mortimer retainer. And it included a bequest of 'my basnet that was my lord Umfree'.[77] So a treasured piece of armour was a gift from a de Bohun, and an executor was a Mortimer man. At the end of the Clanvowe line – for Sir Thomas had no son – the connection to the March of Wales, to the de Bohuns and the Mortimers, which his ancestor Sir Hywel ap Meurig would have recognised before all else, was not forgotten.

There was, however, one more Clanvowe of whom we should take account. This was Perryne, Sir Thomas's wife. She was born Perryne Whitney, daughter of Sir Robert Whitney of Whitney on Wye very near to the border with Brycheiniog, and only a few miles away from the Clanvowe residence at Hergest. Sir Robert had inherited the family estates by 1361, and it may be to the 1360s that we should look for Perryne's date of birth.[78]

She certainly entered the service of Richard II's young queen, Anne of Bohemia at some point before 1390 when the king made her a grant of an annuity of £10 for life, 'for good service to the queen'.[79] Richard and Anne were married in 1382 when both were 15 years old, and it is possible that Perryne was installed in Anne's household shortly afterwards. By the time of the grant of her annuity she was clearly a well-established companion to the queen. It would seem that Perryne remained in Queen Anne's household until the early 1390s. Her departure from the court seems to have coincided with her marriage to Thomas Clanvowe. The pattern of grants to Thomas and Perryne emerges from a series of entries on the Patent Rolls for the years following 1390.

On 28 October 1391 there is a record of grant for life of 40 marks per year to Thomas Clanvowe, the king's esquire. But a note on the roll reveals that the grant was rendered void by surrender, and was cancelled, because the king granted to Thomas and Perryne his wife £20 per year for their lives from the farm of the castle and cantref of Builth and to the said Thomas the said 40 marks from the same fee farm on 12 August in his (the king's) eighteenth year. The last phrase presumably means the eighteenth regnal year of Richard II, which gives a date of 12 August 1394 for the king's re-grant.

The Patent Roll for 1392 contains further information. There are entries recording two grants for 2 October. In one the king grants to Thomas Clanvowe and his wife Perryne, in survivorship (i.e. jointly, but continuing to the end of the life of the one who survives the longer) on their marriage, the sum of £10. This suggests that the grant was made on the occasion of the marriage. The grant was voided and cancelled in similar words to those which were added to Thomas's 1391 grant. The second grant of 2 October 1392 simply replaces Perryne's grant of 1390 with a joint grant to Thomas, esquire of the king, and Perryne, his wife, one of the damsels of the queen's chamber, of an annuity of £10. It is recorded on the roll that Perryne had consented to the replacement, and that the letters patent relating to the 1390 grant had been surrendered. The result of this sequence of transactions was that Thomas and Perryne jointly held an annuity in survivorship of £20, while Thomas held an annuity for life of 40 marks. In other words, the newly married Clanvowes were set up in some state by royal annuities which have to be added to the estates in Herefordshire and the March which they already had or were to inherit on the death of Sir John Clanvowe. It is of interest that from 1394 the annuities were to come from the revenues of Builth, that castle and lordship which had featured so often in the story of Hywel ap Meurig and his family. The favours of the court did not stop in 1394, for in March of 1397 Thomas and Perryne were granted two tuns of wine per year for life.

It seems that both Thomas and Perryne had enjoyed the favour of the king and queen. This in turn raises the question of how they had moved into the court circle. In the case of Thomas, the answer is fairly easy, as he was the son or a close relative of Sir John Clanvowe, who was prominent in the king's service and esteem. Sir John almost certainly introduced Thomas into the king's court. In the case of Perryne, the situation was somewhat similar. Her father, Sir Robert Whitney, was also a man of the court, noted as 'a King's knight' in 1393. The two families were close neighbours in Herefordshire, Sir Robert Whitney's house at Whitney on Wye lying close to the core estates of the Clanvowes, whose manors at Hergest and Yazor were less than ten miles distant to the north and east respectively from Whitney. The Whitneys and the Clanvowes moved in the same circles in Herefordshire. It is entirely likely that Thomas and Perryne knew each other as children, while their presence at court in the 1380s may have brought them even closer. The marriage brought two of the leading families of western Herefordshire into close alliance and buttressed the regional ascendancies of both. Thomas, as we have seen, had made a smooth transition from support for Richard II to a position of trust under Richard's opponent and successor Henry IV. After Thomas had been captured by Owain Glyn Dŵr's forces in 1402, and his muniments lost in the looting and destruction that followed, Henry IV confirmed the previous grants made to him and to Perryne, for a payment of two marks (£1 6s. 8d).

Further letters issued in 1405 to both Thomas and Perryne both re-confirmed the previous grants and acknowledged the difficulties which had beset the couple as a result of the Glyn Dŵr insurrection: destruction at Builth had made the annuities difficult to raise, and Thomas's lands and lordships adjoining Wales had been similarly destroyed.[80] The fading of the insurrection as the decade went on may well have brought the couple some relief, but Perryne faced a new challenge with the death of her husband in 1410. In 1414 she felt it necessary to obtain a confirmation of the grants formerly made to her and Thomas in survivorship at a cost of one hundred shillings paid into the Hanaper. In her widowhood she remained alert to her rights. She acted as plaintiff in an action brought in the court of Chancery against one Hugh Hergest in a case over lands.[81]

It seems, however, that Perryne was far from destitute in the last years of her life. This is revealed by the survival of her will from 1422. The will is a most illuminating document about Perryne's life and personality, and so is given here in full.[82]

IN the name of þe fader and of the son And of þe Holygost, Amen. The thridde day of Aprill In þe зer off our lord M¹ CCCC xxij. I. Peryne Clanbowe, beyng in good memory, thenkyng on my laste ende, hauyng gode in forsyght, I haue maad and ordened this my present testament and my last wylle in þe forme þat foloweth. First I bequeth and commend my saule to gode my maker and my sauyour, and to hys blyssyd moder gloriouse Vyrgyn, And to aH saintes, and my body to be beryed at ʒasore,[83] be my lord my housbond, If I. dye in Hertfordshire,[84] and ellis where þat gode hath ordeined for me, And as son as yt may be doñ godly after þat I hame dede, porelych[85] to be beryed, with-oute gret cost doon thervppoñ. Also I wiH And ordeine þat aH my dettes þat mowe [may] be prowede be good conscience due, þat they be principaly payde in aH þe hast þat it may be.* [? MS. has mayle.] Also I bequeth, to cloth wyth ijc. poormen, xx. H. Also I bequeth to amende brygges[86] and foule wayes x. H. Also I bequeth to Sir Robert of Whitney, my brother, a flate basyn and an ewer, and vj disshes, vj saucers, and ij chargours of seluer [silver]. Also I bequeth to þe same Robert a westment of rede cloth of gold with my massbooke and Chalys: The wych vesseH, vestement, massbooke, and chalys aforseyd, to þe forsaide Roberd bequetheñ, I wole þat [he] haue hem [them] vpoñ this condicion, þat he be good frend to my executours, and þat he lete hem note off ministracion off myn other goode on the Manere of PychardisokeH [Ocle Pychard] ne elles where. Also I bequeth to myn Aunte, prioresse of Lynebroke, xl s'. Also I bequeth to myn Awnte Corbet, xl s'. Also I bequeth to sir Ion Skydmore,[87] my newewe,[88] a girdeH of peerles. Also I bequeth to Lane myn nece, to her mariage, or when sche is of age, xx Hi. Also I bequeth to Peryne her suster, my god doutghter in þe same forme, x Hi; and if it so be þat þe forsaid Iane and Peryne dye be-for þat thay come to age, or ellys maried, then I wiH þat þe mony of either of hem so deede, turn to þe vse of her susters ouerlyuyng [surviving] in þe same fourme. and if aH þe susters dye ar[89] they come to age or be maryed, þat then þe mony tourn to þe vse of her bretheren ouerlyuyng. And if aH þe bretheryn die with-In age of xvj. ʒeere, then þe mony be disposed in Almasdeddes[90] be my executours. Also I be-queeth to Iankyn Myles my seruaunt, xxHi./, and myn eche daies gowne of marterount.[91] Also I bequeth to sir Iohan Coyle, I pare bedes of coraH. Also I bequeth to Elizabeth Ioye .x. Hi. and a booke of Englyssh, cleped 'pore caytife,'[92] and I gown furred with gret menyvere.[93] Also I bequeth to Ionet Okbourn .x març and my sauter helid with blake, and a gown furred with Cristy gray. Also I bequeth to John Huchecoke, v marc. Also I bequeth to Iankyñ Tailour, v març. Also I bequeth to Dauid Morys, xl s'. Also I bequeth to Iohn Hergest, xl s'. Also I bequeth to Luysote xl s'. Also I bequeth to the wyffe of Iankyn' Miles a gown furred with Besshe.[94] Also I bequeth to Dauid Cradoke xiij s' iiij d. Also I bequeth to Iames and to his wyfe x s'. Also I bequeth to þe chirch of ʒasore, fore my lord and his auncetres, to serue in þe chirch, a peire vestimentis of blake, wherof þe same Chirch hath þe cope. Also I bequeth to what thenge[95] þat is most necessary in þe same Chirch, v. març. Also I bequeth to Ionet Knolles a stondyng cuppe of siluer gilte couered. Also I bequeth to Thomas Knolles þe ȝongger a cuppe of siluer gilt couered. Also I bequeth to Iohn Thomas a cuppe of siluer playñ. with þe scripture of seynt Ion. Also I bequeth to two prestes, honest men and good liues, and ellys not,[96] to do diuine seruise for my lord and me. for on ȝer anoon After my decees, resonable lyuelode after þe discrecioun of myñ executours. Also I bequeth to sir Reynold, my prest, iiij. quayres of Doctours on Mathewe. The Residue for soth of all my goodes in this my testament not bequethen, I ȝeue and bequethe to myn executours, be her[97] discrecion to be disposyde, that oon halfe to my pore tenauntz, and þat other halfe to god men faithfull and nedy þat ben in disese.[98] And to þe execucion of this my testament and my last will to be fulfilled, I ordeyn my trusty frendes, Iankyn Miles, Thomas Knolles aforsaid, Elizabeth Ioy, Ionet Okborne, and Iohn Tailour, myne executours be thees presentes, that they will do her[99] besynesse to fulfyll goddes will and myne, as they woll aunsuer afor gode. also I bequeth to ich of myn executours takyng charge of ministracion of this my testament, v. març, and reward for her costages whan they labour specially for my maters. Into wytnessyng of which thyng, to this my present testament I haue put to my seell: ȝeueñ at London, day, moneth, and ȝer, aforsayd.

The significant sums of money and valuables bequeathed by Perryne are interesting suggestions of her wealth: she specified money bequests totalling over £130, to which were added several bequests of silver, silver gilt, fine clothing and jewels. Her reference to her tenants is a reminder that she had presumably received dower after her husband died, and suggests that this was an extensive landed estate for her lifetime.

Her concern for the poor, for men who had fallen on hard times and for her poor tenants suggests something of the continuing effects of the Glyn Dŵr insurgency in the western region of Herefordshire, but more than that it reveals something of Perryne's personality. She seems to have possessed a very practical generosity of spirit. She eschewed the more ostentatious forms of religiosity, as her instructions for a simple burial reveal,[100] while remaining personally pious. Her rejection of funeral pomp, marked by an insistence that she was 'porelych to be beryed, with-oute gret cost doon thervppoñ' and her concern for the moral rectitude of the 'two prestes, honest men and good liues,

and ellys not,[101] to do diuine seruise for my lord and me' both suggest strongly that she may well have shared some of the attitudes of
the Lollards, without necessarily accepting all of the doctrines of the
sect. The emphasis on austerity and on the idea that the fact that they
belonged to the priesthood was of itself no guarantee of the efficacy
of priests' ministrations both hint at Lollard sympathies. It is now
fairly well established that the Pore Caitif tract which was amongst her
bequests is hardly to be counted as an indication of Lollardy.[102] On the
other hand, her will manifests several of the characteristics of Lollard
attitudes including 'the same strain of essentially lay piety which could
so easily turn to support for lollard doctrines.'[103]

Bequests to her brother Sir Robert Whitney and to Sir John
Scudamore suggest the Herefordshire gentry circles in which she
moved, and yet like her husband and many of his ancestors Perryne
had had experience of a world beyond her native region. Her will
indeed suggests similarities with the queen whose companion she had
been. Anne of Bohemia's sympathy for pregnant women and for the
poor generally had established her as a friend of the common people;
her mercy missions in commoners' clothing became the stuff of story,
as did her apparent protection of Wycliffe. It remains possible that
Perryne Whitney had a part in shaping those characteristics. What
is evident is that for the first time it is possible to establish something
of the deeds and the character of one of the women of the family of
Hywel ap Meurig. She represents the end of the line, but also shows
that spirit which enabled her husband's ancestors to develop distinguished careers from their base along the Anglo-Welsh borderland.

And yet there is perhaps a deeper significance to Perryne Clanvowe.
Her father, Sir Robert Whitney, sheriff of Herefordshire and the king's
knight, was responsible for a petition to Parliament in 1378 seeking
remedy for the ravages committed by Welsh malefactors in the county
as far as Hereford itself.[104] The same Sir Robert was to be killed by
Glyn Dŵr's forces at Pilleth in 1402. He had been a member of the
company of the de Bohun earl of Hereford, but the earl, the last of
his line, had died in 1373. So passed one of the great families of the
old March. Another of them, the Mortimers, would come to an end
in 1424. The world of the March was changing. Perryne's husband,
Sir Thomas Clanvowe, was to be captured by the same forces that

killed his father-in-law, and though he was ransomed his estates in the border region were devastated and he and Perryne were forced to live in much reduced circumstances. Perryne's family house at Whitney on Wye was right on the Herefordshire–Brycheiniog border, as was her husband's house at Hergest. But it is perhaps significant that the main focus of Sir Thomas and his ancestors had shifted to Yasor, some miles to the east and closer to Hereford. There is no evidence that Perryne had moved easily amongst the Welsh population to the west. Her youth and young adulthood had been at the English court, her reading matter was English, her language English. As far as we can see, her experiences of the Welsh were as the 'other'. The tendency of the Clanvowes to move away from a focus on Wales to one on England and even beyond England was confirmed by Thomas Clanvowe's choice of Perryne as a wife. They both lived, indeed, in a period when both the March and the principality of Wales, once such fertile ground for the advancement of her husband's family, had largely been abandoned in favour of what were surely seen as more congenial and rewarding opportunities for advancement in England.

Notes

1 Griffiths, *Principality of Wales*, p. 103.
2 *Calendar of Papal Letters* iii, p. 533.
3 *Calendar of Patent Rolls, 1354–58*, p. 101.
4 *Calendar of Charter Rolls, 1341–1417*, p. 132.
5 *Calendar of Patent Rolls, 1361–64*, p. 123, records the presentation in 1361 of William Nicol to the church of Llanfair Llwythyfnwg, in the king's gift by reason of the nonage of the heir of John Clanvowe, who held by knight service of the heir of Roger Mortimer, late earl of March. Llanfair Llwythyfnwg was Gladestry, and this episode indicates that the family maintained its dominant position within that manor.
6 Seymour, 'Sir John Clanvowe', p. 36.
7 McFarlane, *Lancastrian Kings and Lollard Knights*, pp. 231–2.
8 See for cautionary comment, ibid., p. 231.
9 This in spite of the fact that the earl's predecessor had been responsible for a sustained legal onslaught on John's relative Philip ap Rhys. See above, pp. 62–3. For his position in the entourage of the earl of Hereford see Seymour, 'Sir John Clanvowe', p. 38, and *Calendar of Patent Rolls, 1370–74*, p. 325. This last is a record of an *inspeximus* of a grant by Humphrey

de Bohun, late earl of Hereford, Essex and Northampton, dated January 1373, to his bachelor, John Clanvowe, *chivaler*, of a rent of £40 per year out of the manor of Upavon. George Holmes, *The Estates of the Higher Nobility in Fourteenth-Century England*, p. 70, has Clanvowe (Clanevough) as Claverough, which he mistakenly equates with Clavering (index, p. 168). But Holmes's insistence that the silence of records about whether a man was retained by a lord or not is inconclusive is salutary.

[10] Seymour, 'Sir John Clanvowe', pp. 37–9 provides a useful summary. Of particular importance is his comment at p. 37 that 'the records which report his presence in France here and there en passant may not relate the totality of his engagement on land or even perhaps at sea.'

[11] *Calendar of Patent Rolls, 1370–74*, pp. 301, 303.

[12] *Calendar of Close Rolls, 1377–81*, p. 452 where parallel grants to Sir William Neville and Clanvowe are recorded; *Calendar of Patent Rolls, 1381–85*, p. 8 recording the grant of the annuity from the issues of the lordship of Haverford.

[13] *Calendar of Patent Rolls, 1381–85*, p. 104.

[14] *Calendar of Patent Rolls, 1385–89*, pp. 8, 14, 33.

[15] Ibid., p. 379.

[16] *Calendar of Patent Rolls, 1381–85*, p. 285.

[17] *Calendar of Patent Rolls, 1381–85*, p. 17.

[18] See Seymour, 'Sir John Clanvowe', p. 44, where, however, Sir John's employment in the pacification of Wales is not noticed.

[19] *Calendar of Patent Rolls, 1381–85*, p. 575.

[20] For Lawrence and Audley, see Griffiths, *Principality of Wales*, pp. 116–17.

[21] M. Jones, *Ducal Brittany, 1364–1399* (Oxford: University Press, 1970), pp. 184 n. 3, 186.

[22] Seymour, 'Sir John Clanvowe', p. 44. See p. 83.

[23] See Thomas Carte, *Catalogue des Rolles Gascons, Normans et Francois II* (London, 1763), pp. 151–61, providing a good variety of the tasks undertaken by Sir John in the late 1380s.

[24] Ibid., pp. 50–1.

[25] The expedition and its origin of this crusade are discussed by the 'Westminster' continuation of Ranulf Higden's *Polychronicon*. Here the chronicler describes the group of English notables who joined the crusade (from J. R. Lumby, *Polychronicon Ranulphi Higden* (London: Rolls Series, 9 vols, 1865–86), vol. 9, p. 234 (my translation)): 'many noble lords, knights and stout squires from England sought from the king permission to set out in order to bring help to that place [a Christian fortress besieged by Muslim forces in north Africa] amongst them some well-known people, that is the earl of Devon, Sir William Neville, Sir John Clanvowe, and the Master of the Hospital of St John …'

26 Seymour, 'Sir John Clanvowe', p. 52.

27 Siegrid Düll, A. Luttrell and Maurice Keen, 'Faithful unto death: the tomb slab of Sir William Neville and Sir John Clanvowe, Constantinople 1391', *Antiquaries Journal*, 71 (1991), 174–90, at p. 180.

28 A passage from the Westminster chronicle, quoted ibid., describes how after Clanvowe died Neville, inconsolably stricken with grief, did not take any food, and died within two days. It is of course possible that this was merely a dramatic interpretation by retainers of Clanvowe and Neville of the demise of the latter if he and Sir John had been stricken by the same fatal disease.

29 There is a very sound discussion of this episode by Seymour, 'Sir John Clanvowe', pp. 40–1.

30 For sceptical discussion, see ibid., p. 42. In spite of this, a Clanvowe attribution of the poem persists: see, for example, Michael Livingston and John K. Bollard (eds), *Owain Glyndŵr: A Casebook* (Liverpool University Press, 2013), p. 376 (notes to 'The Chronicle of Owain Glyndŵr'): 'Though [J. E.] Lloyd, in accord with scholarly opinion at the time, identifies Sir Thomas Clanvowe as the author of *The Cuckoo and the Nightingale*, it is more likely that the author of this Middle English poem was John Clanvowe, who died in 1392.'

31 See, for example, W. W. Skeat, *The Chaucer Canon* (Oxford: The Clarendon Press, 1900), p. 107: 'the writer may very well have been Sir Thomas Clanvowe, who was a well-known character at the court of Henry IV ...'

32 G. L. Kittredge, 'Chaucer and some of his friends', *Modern Philology*, 1 (June 1903), 1–18, at p. 13.

33 Ibid., p. 18.

34 Ethel Seaton, *Sir Richard Roos* (London, 1961), at pp. 390–2.

35 William McColly, 'The "Book of Cupid" as an Imitation of Chaucer: a Stylo-Statistical View', *The Chaucer Review*, 18/3 (Winter 1984), 239–49.

36 Ibid., pp. 239–40.

37 Ibid., p. 248.

38 Available online at *https://d.lib.rochester.edu/teams/text/symons-chaucerian-dream-visions-and-complaints-boke-of-cupide-introduction*. For the edited text, see *https://d.lib.rochester.edu/teams/text/symons-chaucerian-dream-visions-and-complaints-boke-of-cupide* (both accessed 8 September 2020).

39 M. C. Seymour, 'Sir John Clanvowe 1341–1391', *Transactions of the Radnorshire Society*, 75 (2005), 35–58, at p. 42.

40 Ibid.

41 Ibid., pp. 49–50. See also John Scattergood, 'The date of Sir John Clanvowe's "The Two Ways" and the "Reinvention of Lollardy"', *Medium Aevum*, 79/1 (2010), 116–20.

42 Indeed, Clanvowe's participation in a crusade ran counter to the distaste in which such things were held by many Lollards. As Kightly notes,

'Clanvowe's heresy, like his treatise, seems full of contradictions. We must remember, however, that in these early days of lollardy, attitudes had not yet hardened to the extent which they had done in, say, 1414: it would have been quite possible for Clanvowe to hold some lollard beliefs while rejecting others.' (Charles Kightly, 'The Early Lollards' (unpublished PhD thesis, York University, 1975), p. 192). The simple assumption of Clanvowe's 'heresy' in this passage may perhaps be questioned.

43 McFarlane, *Lancastrian Kings and Lollard Knights*, pp. 148–226 remains unsurpassed as a treatment of those knights close to Richard II's court who were suspected of Lollard beliefs.

44 Kightly, 'Early Lollards', p. 199.

45 McFarlane, *Lancastrian Kings and Lollard Knights*, p. 148. The accusation of Lollardy comes in Thomas Walsingham's *Historia Anglicana*, ii, 159: *Erant autem milites qui hanc sectam coluerunt quam maxime et sustenaverunt, Willelmus Nevile, Lodowicus Clifford, Johannes Clanvowe, Ricardus Stiry, Thomas Latymer, et, inter caeteros major fatuus, Johannes Mountagu.* [There were knights who promoted this sect as much as they could, and sustained it, William Neville, Lewys Clifford, John Clanvowe, Richard Sturry, Thomas Latimer and, the most foolish amongst the others, John Montague.]

46 For the grant of mourning livery to Clanvowe, see TNA E 101/401/16. For the appointments of executors in Joan of Kent's will, see N. H. Nicolas, *Testamenta Vetusta* (London, 1826), pp. 15–17.

47 Ibid.

48 See pp. 75, 95; McFarlane, *Lancastrian Kings and Lollard Knights*, p. 230.

49 G. A. Holmes, *The Estates of the Higher Nobility in Fourteenth-Century England* (Cambridge: Cambridge University Press, 1957), pp. 60–4.

50 Seymour, 'Sir John Clanvowe', p. 44.

51 *Calendar of Patent Rolls, 1381–85*, pp. 587–8.

52 See Sir N. Harris Nicolas, *The Controversy Sir Richard Scrope and Sir Robert Grosvenor in the Court of Chivalry A.D. MCCCLXXXV–MCCCLX* (London, 1832), pp. 438–9.

53 For Sir John's service alongside Beauchamp, see *Rotuli Parliamentorum*, II, pp. 326–7 (1376); Seymour, 'Sir John Clanvowe', pp. 40–1 (1380); *Testamenta Vetusta*, I, pp. 14–15 (1386); Seymour, 'Sir John Clanvowe', p. 50 (1388); T. Carte (ed.), *Rotuli Francie* (London, 1743), II, p. 161 (1390).

For his service alongside Sir William Neville, see *Rotuli Parliamentorum*, II, pp. 326–7 (1376); Seymour, 'Sir John Clanvowe', p. 40 n. 23 (1377/8); Seymour, 'Sir John Clanvowe', pp. 40–1 (1380); *Testamenta Vetusta*, I, p. 109 (1380); *Calendar of Close Rolls, 1377–81*, p. 452 (1381); *Rotuli Scotiae*, II, p. 75 (1385); *Calendar of Patent Rolls, 1385–89*, p. 72 (1385); *Testamenta Vetusta*, I, pp. 14–15 (1386); *Calendar of Patent Rolls, 1385–9*, p. 214 (1386); Seymour, 'Sir John Clanvowe', p. 47 (1387); Lumby (ed.), *Higden,*

Polychronicon, IX, pp. 234, 240 (1390); Seymour, 'Sir John Clanvowe', pp. 52–3 (1391).

54 T. F. Tout, *Chapters in the Administrative History of Medieval England IV* (Manchester: The University Press, 1928), p. 178.

55 For Scudamore as a colleague of Sir John, see, for example, *Calendar of Patent Rolls 1388–92*, p. 217, when the two were members of a commission investigating the lands of the late John Hastings which were in the king's hands in 1390. For Scudamore's appointment in 1399 alongside Sir Thomas as an attorney of Richard Kyngeston, clerk, going to Ireland, see *Calendar of Patent Rolls, 1396–99*, p. 520. Walter Devereux was named as a friend of Sir John in 1390: *Calendar of Patent Rolls 1388–92*, p. 361; he or his son, also Walter, served with Sir Thomas as a justice of the peace for Herefordshire in 1397: *Calendar of Patent Rolls, 1396–99*, p. 227.

56 Thus Sir Thomas witnessed the transfer of the castle and lordship of Ewyas Harold to William Beauchamp in 1400: *Calendar of Close Rolls, 1399–1402*, p. 116.

57 See the previous note.

58 *Testamenta Vetusta*, I, p. 165.

59 There is an excellent survey of Sir Thomas's official career by Charles Kightly: 'Clanvowe, Thomas (d. 1410) of Hergest and Yazor, Herefs', in J. S. Roskill, L. Clark and C. Rawcliffe (eds), *The History of Parliament: The House of Commons 1386–1421* (Woodbridge: Boydell and Brewer, 1993); this can be consulted online, at *https://www.historyofparliamentonline.org/volume/1386-1421/member/clanvowe-thomas-1410* (accessed 16 August 2020).

60 Ibid.

61 Ibid.

62 Ibid.

63 *Calendar of Patent Rolls, 1399–1401*, p. 53.

64 Kightly, 'Clanvowe, Thomas'.

65 *Calendar of Patent Rolls, 1401–5*, p. 128. The Herefordshire commission appointed alongside Sir Thomas included men with strong Clanvowe associations, such as William Beauchamp, baron Abergavenny, and Walter Devereux, for whom see notes 55 and 56 above.

66 For Sir Kinard de la Bere as a friend of Sir John Clanvowe in 1290, see *Calendar of Patent Rolls, 1288–92*, p. 361.

67 J. E. Lloyd, *Owen Glendower* (Oxford: The Clarendon Press, 1931), p. 151.

68 See note 71 below.

69 Lloyd, *Owen Glendower*, p. 59.

70 See Ralph A. Griffiths, 'Owain Glyn Dŵr's invasion of the central March of Wales in 1402: the evidence of clerical taxation', *Studia Celtica*, 46 (2012), 111–22. Amongst the churches devastated was that of Gladestry, a place which had a long association with the family of Sir Thomas.

71 *Calendar of Patent Rolls, 1401–5*, p. 170.

72 Ibid., p. 392.

73 Kightly, 'Clanvowe, Thomas'.

74 Kightly, 'Early Lollards', p. 198.

75 Ibid.

76 Ibid. See further notes 92, 102 below.

77 Kightly, 'Clanvowe, Thomas'. For Partrich, see Holmes, *Estates of the Higher Nobility*, p. 62.

78 For Sir Robert Whitney, see the summary by Charles Kightly in the *History of Parliament*, available online at *https://www.historyofparliamentonline.org/ volume/1386-1421/member/whitney-sir-robert-i-1402*.

79 *Calendar of Patent Rolls, 1388–92*, p. 250.

80 *Calendar of Patent Rolls, 1405–8*, p. 94.

81 London, TNA C 1/16/78.

82 The following text relies heavily on that published by Frederick J. Furnivall, *The Fifty Earliest English Wills in the Court of Probate, London, A.D. 1387–1439*, EETS [Original Series] 78 London, 1882), 50.

83 Yazor.

84 Herefordshire.

85 Simply, without ostentation.

86 Bridges.

87 Sir John Scudamore of Kentchurch, Herefordshire (who married the daughter of Owain Glyndŵr), or his son and namesake.

88 Nephew.

89 Before.

90 Alms.

91 The skin or fur of the marten; see Sherman M. Kuhn (ed.), *Middle English Dictionary Part M.2* (Ann Arbor: University of Michigan Press, 1975), p. 199.

92 The Pore Caitif, a tract with alleged Lollard associations. See Sister Mary Teresa Brady, 'The Pore Caitif: an introductory study', *Traditio*, 10 (1954), 529–48, who reaches the following conclusion (at p. 548): 'About the strongest case that could be made favoring Lollard associations must rest on the fact that The Pore Caitif appears in manuscripts which contain Wycliffite works, and that it incorporates quotations from Grosseteste, Abuile and Peraldus (or one of his descendants), three men whose works were frequently quoted in Lollard tracts. If the Pore Caitif is a Lollard tract, it is a unique one, without, apparently, a trace of Lollardy …'

93 Miniver, a white fur from the red squirrel.

94 A dark fur, sometimes of rabbit.

95 Whatever.

96 Nothing else – i.e. nothing other than good, virtuous lives.

[97] By their.

[98] Half to her poor tenants and half to good men in difficulty.

[99] Their.

[100] It should be noted, however, that this, as many other aspects of Perryne's will, relates very closely, sometimes verbatim, to her husband's will. See Kightly, 'Clanvowe, Thomas'.

[101] Nothing else – i.e. nothing other than good, virtuous lives.

[102] See note 92 above, and also Margaret Deanesly, *The Lollard Bible* (Cambridge: Cambridge University Press, 1920) pp. 346–7; Charles Kightly, 'The early Lollards', pp. 197–8, notes that 'Perryne Clanvowe's will has a definitely Lollard flavour, for it is in English (a thing still by no means usual) and it resembles the "Lollard wills" in its lack of funeral masses or other pomp …' This falls some way short of definitively identifying Perryne as a Lollard, but it certainly raises some suspicion that she harboured attitudes that were potentially Lollard.

[103] Knightly, 'Early Lollards', p. 197.

[104] William Rees (ed.), *Calendar of Ancient Petitions relating to Wales* (Cardiff: University of Wales Press, 1975), pp. 166–7.

7

Some Reflections

The story of Meurig ap Philip and his descendants extends over some two hundred years. It ranges from the family's service to great lords in the borderland of Herefordshire and the March to careers that involved high-level political and administrative activity throughout southern Wales, participation in the county politics of Herefordshire while ultimately one line of Meurig's descendants rose to the rarefied heights of the royal court, and an involvement in war and diplomacy across much of Europe and beyond. But even international adventures and a tendency to become entrenched in the politics of Herefordshire, in membership of government commissions in the county, and in representing that county in parliament, could not entirely eradicate the family links with Wales and the March.

While one branch of the family developed as courtiers and diplomats, another rose to the level of Marcher lords in their own right and experienced the vagaries of fame and of fortune that were so often the lot of such magnates. The diverse careers of members of the family saw them sometimes as the faithful servants of the kings of England, and sometimes as rebels who suffered for their opposition to royal governance. But there was more consistency in the family's attachment over several generations to their Mortimer patrons. A similar attachment marks their relationship with the de Bohuns, earls of Hereford and lords of Brecon, with the single and significant exception of the clash of interests which took place in the 1340s and 1350s.

The descendants of Meurig ap Philip are by no means unique in the history of Wales in the medieval centuries. Instead, they are indicative of a trend within Wales that was truly transformative. They represent, and in many respects were harbingers of, the class of Welsh gentry that was coming rapidly to prominence in the later Middle Ages.[1] Most families in this class come into the category of a ministerial aristocracy, which emerged into prominence and wealth from careers of service to Welsh princes and lords, Marcher magnates, or the English kings. They amount to many dozens of families drawn from all parts of Wales and the March and include some men who are already famous in the historiography of Wales in the Middle Ages. Foremost amongst them are the descendants of Ednyfed Fychan, the chief minister of Llywelyn the Great, who included men who were central to the administration of Llywelyn ap Gruffudd, prince of Wales in the third quarter of the thirteenth century, and who included three of Ednyfed's sons.[2] The same family subsequently provided highly significant royal officials such as Sir Gruffudd Llwyd (d. 1335) and Sir Rhys ap Gruffudd (d. 1356), dominant figures in north Wales and south Wales respectively in the fourteenth century.[3] The study of the development of the Welsh gentry class is far from complete. Its origins and growth have been examined for north Wales, and elsewhere in Wales individual families have been very well studied. But for several regions – and they are regions in which the descendants of Meurig ap Philip were markedly active – the emergence and rise of the squirearchy and the gentry have not been given the same study.

What is evident in the case of the family story that has unfolded in the present book is the freedom with which they made transitions from the March into both England and Wales. Their story shows that for those with the wit and good fortune to exploit it this was a more open and more fluid world than is often depicted. A combination of hard work and a willingness to face risks offered a real, if often perilous, chance to forge highly successful careers. Particularly striking is the way in which Hywel ap Meurig and his descendants appear to have nurtured their wealth and advanced the careers of their offspring. The adoption by William ap Hywel's descendants of the Anglicised name of de Clanvowe in place of the Welsh patronymic is a case in point, as is the evident determination of Hywel ap Meurig that several of his sons should go into the church, a move which offered a relatively safe and influential as well as a potentially lucrative career path. The way in which Rees ap Hywel and his son established themselves as

Marcher lords and the apparent ease with which the Clanvowes passed from office-holding in Wales to political service in Herefordshire and thence to the royal court and service overseas are, in their different ways, indicative of the ambition and social agility that characterised the family for several generations. The progress of the Clanvowes also demonstrates not simply the attractions of Herefordshire as a source of administrative eminence and of contacts with members of a county community of fellow landholders, but as a means of access to the royal court itself.

One of the most interesting aspects of the growth of the power and influence of the descendants of Meurig ap Philip is the development of the family estates. The ascent of Rees ap Hywel and Philip ap Rees into the ranks of Marcher lords has already been charted in Chapter 4 above. It was a major advance, which has few parallels in fourteenth-century Welsh history. But additional and sometimes more lasting acquisitions by other family members in Marcher and English locations have attracted less attention.

The first developments of an extended territorial base for Hywel ap Meurig and his descendants took place in the thirteenth century. It is very difficult to establish the extent of the lands held by Hywel ap Meurig. It is very likely that he was responsible for developing the house at Hergest, and may have had a residence at Gladestry, where he acted as reeve for the Mortimer lords – though assuredly not on a regular basis.[4] It is likely, given both his presence at Bronllys in 1271 and the punitive measures subsequently taken against him and his son John by Llywelyn ap Gruffudd, that he had at least one residence within the principality that Llywelyn had constructed and which embraced much of the March.[5] The evidence does not, however, allow us to engage in much more than generalisations and educated guesses.

But with Hywel's sons the situation becomes clearer. Philip, who seems to have been the head of the family following Hywel's death in 1281, certainly possessed a significant residence at Hergest in 1290, when he entertained the bishop of Hereford there.[6] We are able to find significant Herefordshire lands held by Philip ap Hywel in the early fourteenth century. He held the manor of Ocle Pychard, north-east of Hereford, by the service of one knight's fee in 1303.[7] Some thirteen years later Philip ap Hywel is recorded as holding Burghill, a few miles north-west of Hereford, jointly with three others, John of Pembridge, Walter of Burghill and Andrew of Burghill.[8] This would seem to have been an estate acquired by Hywel and his fellows, as it appears in 1303 as being held by Roger de Burghill and Elizabeth Gamage.[9] Somewhat similarly, Philip ap Hywel held Tillington very close to Burghill, in 1316, along with Henry de Burghill and John de Burghill.[10] In 1303 that manor had been in the hands of Roger de Burghill.[11] It seems quite likely that Roger de Burghill was dead by 1316, and that Philip had acquired a share of both Burghill and Tillington, possibly through purchase. By the same date, Philip shares Ocle Pychard with the abbot of Lyra, and also holds Michaelchurch on Arrow.[12] Again, we find Philip ap Hywel holding King's Pyon in 1316, jointly with Gerard of Eylesford and 'Ricardus' ap Hywel. It is tempting to read 'Ricardus' as an erroneous expansion of an original 'R' denoting Philip's brother Rees.[13]

Indeed, in some instances Rees was unambiguously associated with Philip in the acquisition of lands. Thus in 1317 Philip and Rees and Richard de la Lynde hold two-and-three-quarter knights' fees, with an annual value of £36, in *Pyonia* and *Houton Cotes*.[14] In a record of 1332 Philip, Rees (by that date both dead) and Joan Pychard are noted as having held in Stanford Faucon, Staunton, Ocle Pychard and Bishampton (the last in Worcestershire),[15] and in 1336 an inquisition post mortem adds Almeley, Leighton, Michaelchurch (on Arrow) *Manewhiteschirche* in Herefordshire and Upton in Worcestershire to the joint holdings of Philip, Rees and Joan Pychard.[16]

Analysis of the family possession of manors in Herefordshire in the first two decades of the fourteenth century reveals the principal part apparently taken by Philip ap Hywel in the acquisition of Herefordshire lands. He was rivalled in this respect only by his young nephew and eventual heir, Philip de Clanvowe, the son of William ap Hywel.[17] He is described in an extent of the de Bohun lordship of Hay of 1340 as holding the manor of 'Clannogh', from which he presumably derived his surname, by service of a military fee and common suit of court. It would appear that the manor of Clannogh or Clanvowe was amongst the early, probably the earliest of Philip's possessions. One of Philip's acquisitions was the manor of Yazor, the church of which would become in time the family mausoleum. In 1316 Yazor was held by

Sybil de Acton, the dean and chapter of Hereford, and the prior of Llanthony Prima.[18] But a fine of 1318 reveals Richard de Baskerville granting Philip de Clanvowe and his wife Philippa seventy-five acres of woodland. The rest of the manor was in the hands of Sybil de Acton, as her dower provision from her husband. But Richard de Baskerville undertook that, once Sybil was dead, he would hand over the manor in its entirety to Philip and Philippa. It appears that Philip and his wife were to owe to Richard de Baskerville only the token render of a rose on the feast of the Nativity of St John the Baptist (24 June), as well as owing the usual services to the chief lords, initially in respect of the seventy-five acres of woodland and subsequently, after Sybil's death, for the entire manor.[19] The whole transaction perhaps lends support to a speculation that Philippa may have been a member of the Baskerville family.[20] We have seen that Philip de Clanvowe's lands in 1336 included Ocle Pychard, King's Pyon and Yazor in Herefordshire, and in Hergest, Michaelchurch by Huntington, Cusop, *Dolsuleyn* and *Llywenny* in the March.[21] Philip had acquired the manor of King's Pyon – presumably by purchase from Philip ap Hywel and his co-tenants – by the mid-1320s. Consequent upon his apparent failure to repay a loan of two hundred pounds from Edmund, earl of Arundel it seems that the earl took steps to seize the manor of King's Pyon. An early step in this process was to have an extent made of the manor, which proves interesting as an indication of the sort of lands that were being acquired by members of the family in Herefordshire and the March. The extent contains the following information:

> Philip de Clanvowe has in the manor of Kings Pyon Herefords., 80 quarters of wheat worth 3s. a quarter; 36 quarters of oats worth 18d. a quarter; 12 quarters of peas worth 2s. a quarter; 2 carts with iron tyres worth 26s 8d.; a messuage, gardens, vineyard, dovecot, worth 20s a year. Rents of assize worth £9 6s. 8d. Pleas of the court worth 6s. 8d. 180 acres of arable worth 6d an acre a year; 9 acres of meadow worth 2s. a year. Pasture worth 20s a year. Woodland worth half a mark a year.[22]

Many of the manors which were in the sole possession of Philip ap Hywel, such as Hergest, or with which Philip de Clanvowe was associated, such as Yazor and Cusop, appear to have continued in the possession of the Clanvowe branch of the family through much of the fourteenth century.[23] From the pattern of acquisitions described above, two main trends emerge. The first is that Philip, and Rees, appear to have developed a strategy for acquisition that led to their tenure of manors in partnership with others. This may have involved a merging of interests, which enabled the sons of Hywel ap Meurig, at a price, to spread their influence through Herefordshire. Subsequently a more straightforward process may have involved acquisition through marriage – as perhaps in the case of Yazor.

The second aspect of the accumulation of lands by the family is their distribution. It is most interesting that the majority of the lands that we know to have been acquired constituted a belt of properties which lay in an east–west alignment across central Herefordshire. It looks as though the family were being a little more than simply opportunistic in their dealing in lands, and were deliberately constructing a belt of property and associated influence across the county. We have to add to this the lands in Wales assembled by Rees ap Hywel and his son Philip,[24] so we have something very close to a continuum of territory in which the family mixed control and influence, and which extended from the fringes of *pura Wallia* in the west, through the March and then through Herefordshire. If we add to that a number of lands in Worcestershire we can see a significant position of regional influence which cut across the usual structures of governance – lordships and counties – to give the descendants of Hywel ap Meurig a distinct 'presence' across a broad band of territory. For a family that had emerged from a relatively undistinguished background in the Welsh March, this was no mean achievement.

The eminence in Herefordshire of the Clanvowe branch of the family emphasises that in part at least the family story is one of Anglicisation. It is evident that the social milieux within which the family members moved changed over the generations. Hywel ap Meurig seems to have moved easily between Welsh and English communities and colleagues, though his patrons were always English – from the kings, Henry III and Edward I, through to the great lords, Roger Mortimer and Humphrey de Bohun. Much the same was the case with his sons Philip, Master Rees, and William, who had at times some close Welsh associates. Philip and Rees developed political careers which had significant English dimensions, in terms of service on behalf of, or opposition to, the English court, though they often played out in a Welsh context, involving both *pura Wallia* and the March – like involvement in Thomas of Lancaster's eventually fatal opposition to Edward II and the hunt for the king when he became a fugitive. All the while Master Rees was building a life as a Marcher lord, in which he was followed by his son Philip. Whether this gave him a Welsh, or an English, identity – or an amalgam of the two – is hard to know. And the strong possibility that Philip ap Hywel was buried in Hereford cathedral, having been before his death a canon of St Davids and archdeacon of Brecon, merely emphasises the ambiguity in his position.

That ambiguity is fully exemplified in the career of Hywel ap Meurig's grandson Philip Clanvowe, son of William ap Hywel, for he was active in both England and Wales, and his Welsh ancestry was balanced by his predominantly English associates and patrons. For this man of Welsh descent, but with an English-sounding name, was a consistent and trusted official of Edward III in both Wales and Herefordshire and other locations in England, and was able to count men with names such as Grandison, Chandos, Devereux and Lucas amongst his closest colleagues. By the time of the later Clanvowes, we are dealing with men whose focus is on building careers in Herefordshire and beyond, in the English court, which in one case, that of Sir John Clanvowe, will lead to adventures in international diplomacy and crusading. There were still instances when members of this family were engaged in politics and administration in Wales, but this seems to have been undertaken in the interests of English monarchs as well as of self-advancement. That Welsh involvement was, however, always of limited duration and was outweighed in significance by obligations and opportunities in England. It is at once ironic as well as curiously fitting that Sir Thomas, the last of the male Clanvowes, a family who had played no little part in the administration of fourteenth-century Wales, should have been distinguished in the historical record primarily as a prisoner of Owain Glyn Dŵr, after a battle in which his father-in-law and many of his friends had been killed by Glyn Dŵr's forces, and that his fellow captive was a member of the Mortimer dynasty who had for so long been his family's lords and patrons.

Turning now to the women of the family, it is of course the case that we have much less evidence about them than about their husbands and other males. Nevertheless, some observations are possible. We have looked at Perryne Clanvowe, who married into the family, but there were, of course, other examples of survival of women amongst the descendants of Meurig ap Philip. We have already noticed Elizabeth, daughter of Philip ap Rees. Elizabeth married first Sir Henry Mortimer of Chelmarsh and secondly Adam de Peasenhall. Elizabeth's sister Mabel married Hugh Wrottesley. Another Elizabeth was the daughter of Rees ap Rees, and she married Ralph Bluet, a member of a family which had developed landed interests in the March. There was in addition a further Elizabeth, a daughter of Sir Philip Clanvowe, who married into the Poyntz family of Iron Acton in Gloucestershire. It is thought that her effigy is still to be found in the parish church, lying next to that of her husband, Sir John Poyntz. It had been an important marriage – so important that the coat of arms of the Poyntz family, recorded in the heraldic visitation of Gloucestershire in 1623, still bore in its quarterings the coat of arms that Elizabeth de Clanvowe had used, and that had originated with the rise to knightly status of Hywel ap Meurig some century before her death. The important point here is that though we can trace continued involvement in the affairs of Wales on the part of the descendants of Hywel, albeit on a decreasing scale in the case of the Clanvowes, it was in England that the men found wives, and it was in England that their daughters found husbands. The wives and daughters appear in general to have had strikingly English names: Hywel ap Meurig's wife was Matilda; Philip ap Rees was married to a Joan and had daughters Elizabeth and Mabel; his brother Rees ap Rees had a daughter Elizabeth; Philip de Clanvowe's only identifiable wife was Philippa, and his only known daughter was yet another Elizabeth.

It is notable that the name Elizabeth was a favourite in both major branches of the family in the fourteenth century. A similar partiality for a limited number of names can be seen amongst the sons of the family: Philip is a case in point – Hywel ap Meurig's father was Meurig ap Philip; one of Hywel's sons was Philip; William ap Hywel's son was Philip de Clanvowe and Master Rees ap Hywel's son was Philip ap Rees, or sometimes Philip de Bronllys. The Clanvowe line broke away from that pattern, with two sons called John and two named Thomas.[25] The trend amongst the Clanvowes towards names that do not reflect the former family tradition seems significant in that it coincides with the period at which this branch of the family turned increasingly towards England. The turn towards England can be fairly precisely dated and is of considerable significance.

It must be seen first in the context of the fear that the Welsh inspired in the border counties of England in the fourteenth century. In the late 1370s the representatives of Herefordshire in Parliament , together with the sheriff of the county, Sir Robert Whitney, complained that 'Malefactors from Wales have come within these past two years in companies of forty, sixty or one hundred, and there they have beaten people and maimed several; more they have killed in the houses, and taken their chattels, committing such brutalities and threats in the county as far as the city of Hereford that no man dare indict or take them for fear of being killed in their house …'[26] Sir Robert Whitney was, of course, the father of Perryne Whitney, and thus the future father-in-law of Sir Thomas Clanvowe. Both would fight against Glyn Dŵr's men at Pilleth in 1402; Sir Robert would be killed, and Sir Thomas taken captive. More generally the Parliament of 1376 heard complaints of similar depredations on behalf of the counties of Worcester, Shropshire, Staffordshire, Herefordshire and Gloucestershire. By the mid-1340s, Welsh lawlessness and rumours of lawlessness were becoming widespread and English fear of insurrection was growing. In Merioneth the English sheriff was murdered, and the town of Rhuddlan, inhabited in the main by English burgesses, was attacked. And in 1345 Henry Shaldeford, the newly appointed attorney of the Black Prince in north Wales, was set upon and murdered. Well might the burgesses of Denbigh report in terror that 'the Welsh have never been so disposed to rise against their liege lord and to conquer the land from him'.

In such circumstances it is hardly surprising, though very instructive, that members of a family that had experience of working closely with marcher lords and royal officials would take advantage of their contacts with Herefordshire gentry and their extensive network of lands in the same and neighbouring counties to establish themselves rapidly as members of the administrative elite in English county society. At the same time, they appear to have begun to shed their Welshness and to turn their backs on Wales. The process by which the de Bohun earl of Northampton and the earl of Hereford ganged up against Sir Philip ap Rees and relieved him of many of his lordships and powers in the March has, naturally enough, been pictured as an episode of persecution of an emerging magnate of Welsh blood by haughty and avaricious English (de Bohun) marcher lords. And yet Sir Philip was left with the manor of Shifnall, in eastern Shropshire, and with lordship over Talgarth English (and this removed his lordship over Welsh tenantry). The arrangements which Sir Philip subsequently made for the descent of his lands resulted in their passage to the descendants of his niece Elizabeth who had married into the Bluet family.

In spite of their eventual turn towards England in cultural and careerist terms and against their Welsh and Marcher heritage, the members of the family which attained eminence with Hywel ap Meurig left a significant number of monuments to their prominence and their achievement, and sometimes their pride, scattered through the landscapes of Wales and the March. Most impressive are three castles associated with the family. First come the earthen remains, perhaps still concealing much stonework, of the great Edwardian castle of Builth which Hywel ap Meurig did so much to construct, and his descendants did so much to preserve and guard.[27] Just as notable is the surviving tower of Bronllys castle, where what appears to be fourteenth-century additions and reconstructions are reminiscent of the time when members of one branch of the family were lords of that place and the adjoining lordship of Cantref Selyf.[28] A third castle associated with the Clanvowe branch of the family was at Cusop, a manor associated with them from the early fourteenth century. Once again it seems likely that some masonry remains may underlie the present earthworks.[29] But there are also within Herefordshire the now abandoned ruins of the church of St John at Yazor, described by Sir Thomas Clanvowe as 'the place of mine ancestors'.[30] And fragments of the house begun by Hywel ap Meurig in the 1260s at Hergest on the very border of Herefordshire lies within the later buildings from which Hergest Court emerged. It is likely that fourteenth-century additions to churches in areas where the family were significant landholders were the result of their patronage.[31] While being the beneficiaries of the patronage of the Mortimers and the de Bohuns, the descendants of Meurig ap Philip almost certainly became the patrons of others, including their own tenantry and some of their less eminent neighbours, lay and clerical, in Herefordshire. From the evidence currently available it is difficult to identify those who became dependent on, say, Hywel ap Meurig's sons, but the will of Perryne Clanvowe suggests that even in the difficult times following her husband's capture by Glyn Dŵr and the wasting of his lands there were still many who relied on her benevolence. There is therefore almost certainly more to discover about the impact of this remarkable family on their regional environment of the March, on the politics of Wales and of Herefordshire, and of the realm of England and beyond. But what has been recovered in this book already places them amongst the most gifted and important of the families of the March.

More than anything, perhaps, the Clanvowe branch of the family had made a highly significant decision. A key point in their turn eastwards was the period of Sir Philip Clanvowe's deeper involvement in the administration of Herefordshire. This took place in a period when political tensions ran high in some parts of Wales, and it is possible that Sir Philip had attempted to establish himself and his family more securely in a safer region.[32] In the fourteenth century, the family's fortunes lay less with involvement in the west, in *pura Wallia*, or even in the March, but increasingly in the east, in England, in particular in London at the royal court. That future was terminated by a failure of male heirs but, though they cannot have known it, they had foreshadowed a crucial element in the future of Wales for generations to come.[33]

Notes

[1] A. D. Carr, *The Gentry of North Wales in the Later Middle Ages* (Cardiff: University of Wales Press, 2017), especially pp. 28–66 where the importance of careers based on service to the crown is emphasised. For other aspirational families in the Middle March, see R. R. Davies, *Lordship and Society in the March of Wales*, pp. 225–6, a masterly survey of the descendants of Einion Sais in the lordship of Brecon in the same period as the family of Hywel ap Meurig. But the 'trajectory' of the descendants was altogether more local than that of those of Hywel ap Meurig.

[2] See Stephenson, *Political Power in Medieval Gwynedd*, pp. 102–6.

[3] For Sir Gruffudd Llwyd, see J. G. Edwards, 'Sir Gruffydd Llwyd', *English Historical Review*, 30 (1915), 589–601, and the splendid survey

of J. Beverley Smith, 'Gruffudd Llwyd, Sir', in the *Oxford Dictionary of National Biography*. For Sir Rhys ap Gruffudd, see the invaluable summary in Griffiths, *Principality of Wales*, pp. 99–102.

4 *Calendar of Inquisitions, Miscellaneous, II (1308–48)*, p. 404 no. 1643. See also p. 7.

5 See above, pp. 15–19.

6 See above, p. 35.

7 *Inquisitions and Assessments relating to Feudal Aids*, vol. 2 (London: HMSO, 1900), p. 379.

8 Ibid., p. 385.

9 Ibid., p. 376.

10 Ibid., p. 386.

11 Ibid., p. 376.

12 Ibid., p. 390.

13 Ibid., p. 387. On the other hand, there was a Richard ap Hywel who appeared prominently in documents of a slightly earlier date relating to Pipton, a manor adjacent to Bronllys: see Wells-Furby, *Catalogue of the Medieval Muniments at Berkeley Castle*, II, pp. 665: C2/1/7 (1309), C2/1/8 (1311). He also appears in documents relating to Porthaml, ibid., C2/1/10 (1306); and Talgarth, ibid., p. 667: C2/2/1 (1299). It is possible that this Richard ap Hywel was a little older than the man of, apparently, the same name who shared King's Pyon with Philip ap Hywel.

14 *Calendar of Close Rolls 1313–18*, p. 419.

15 *Calendar of Inquisitions Post Mortem, II, 1327–77*, p. 284. The text is incomplete, and may be reconstituted by reference to the record of 1336, for which see the following note.

16 Ibid., p. 496.

17 See above, p. 69.

18 *Inquisitions and Assessments relating to Feudal Aids*, vol. 2, p. 386.

19 TNA CP 25/1/82/33, no. 137.

20 This is perhaps the most tempting explanation for what appears to have been Richard de Baskerville's generosity. See for other possible marriages of Philip de Clanvowe, p. 76. It should be noted that it is possible that Philip de Clanvowe's acquisition of Yazor may have been significantly more complex than is suggested by the fine cited in the previous note. A debt of £400 owed by Sir Philip Clanvowe to Sir John de Aston who formerly held the fee of Yazor suggests subsequent stages in the transfer of the fee to Philip Clanvowe. See TNA C 241/117/25.

21 *Calendar of Charter Rolls, 1327–41*, p. 352; *Calendar of Inquisitions Post Mortem, II, 1327–77*, p. 496.

22 TNA, C 131/2/16. The manor was almost certainly never taken into the earl of Arundel's possession: in the turmoil that followed the return of

Roger Mortimer to England with Queen Isabella in 1326 Arundel was commissioned by the king to raise troops but was seized at Shrewsbury by his enemy John Charlton of Powys and taken to Hereford where on 17 November of 1326 he was executed at the instance of Roger Mortimer.

23 See pp. 75, 95, 118.

24 See above, Chapter 4.

25 Sir Thomas was the last of the male line of the Clanvowes; for Thomas son of Philip Clanvowe, see p. 82.

26 William Rees (ed.), *Calendar of Ancient Petitions relating to Wales* (Cardiff: University of Wales Press, 1975), pp. 166–7.

27 The site of Builth castle is perhaps the least investigated of all the castles constructed on the orders of Edward I; in view of the recurrent role of Meurig ap Philip's descendants, the surviving remains stand as a memorial to the family. It has to be a possibility that some stone elements survive under the earthen mounds and embankments that survive.

28 See pp. 59–60, 63.

29 The scheduling report on Cusop Castle includes the following comments: 'Although no longer visible above ground, nineteenth-century records of standing fabric including a gateway, and later references to masonry foundations, suggest that Cusop Castle included buildings constructed from stone, the buried remains of which will survive. The ringwork is one of a number of medieval defensive sites located in strategic positions above the Wye Valley, the land belonging to the King at the time of Domesday survey. The castle is believed to have been constructed by the Cianowes or Clarowes family who were prominent in the county during the 12th to 14th centuries.' The references to the 'Cianowes or Clarowes' of course are to the Clanvowes.

30 There seems to have been early fourteenth-century rebuilding of this church, where the windows 'indicate an early C14 date' (Brooks and Pevsner, *Herefordshire*, p. 692). This coincides neatly with the acquisition of Yazor by Philip de Clanvowe, which began *c*.1318.

31 The dedication of two altars in the church of King's Pyon in April 1329 is particularly interesting. The altars may have been the result of pious donations by the successors of the brothers Philip and Rees, or by the brothers themselves. Philip had died in January 1329, and Rees by May 1328. See above, pp. 44–5 and 57. See also Bannister (ed.), *Registrum Ade de Orleton*, p. 339. There is also much late-thirteenth-century and early-fourteenth-century work at Kington, the church that served Hergest. See Brooks and Pevsner, *Herefordshire*, pp. 398–9.

32 For the tensions of the 1340s, see the brief summary in R. R. Davies, *The Age of Conquest: Wales 1063–1415* (Oxford: Oxford University Press, 2000), p. 411, where the murder of Henry Shaldeford, the Black Prince's attorney,

in February 1345 is described as 'the climax of anti-English violence in north Wales in the 1340s, which had already included the murder of the sheriff of Merioneth, the seizure of his records and a riotous assault on the town and castle of Rhuddlan.' By 1346, when Sir Philip was once more charged with duties in South Wales it is interesting that the Black Prince was showing signs of increasing annoyance that he was so ill-supplied with revenues from that region: see *Register of Edward the Black Prince Part I A.D. 1346–1348*, pp. 4–5. There is a distinct sense of nervousness about the state of governance in much of Wales in the mid-1340s.

[33] See Emrys Jones (ed.), *The Welsh in London 1500–2000* (Cardiff: University of Wales Press on behalf of The Honourable Society of Cymmrodorion, 2001).

Appendix
Meurig and William,
Sons of Rees ap Meurig

William ap Rees was enfeoffed by Edward II with the lordship of Talgarth in 1312. William subsequently re-granted it to two of the sons and a grandson of Hywel ap Meurig: Philip ap Hywel, Rees ap Hywel, and Philip de Bronllys, this last also known as Philip ap Rees ap Hywel. William's grant was made to them and the issue of Philip de Bronllys, with remainder to John de Bronllys, brother of Philip de Bronllys and his issue, remainder to James de Bronllys, and his issue, remainder to Elizabeth de Bronllys and her issue, and final remainder to the right heirs of Rees ap Hywel. In other words, William ap Rees was acting in the interests of Rees ap Hywel and his family. If William ap Rees could be identified as a brother of Philip ap Rees it would suggest that Rees ap Hywel may have had yet another son, Meurig, a brother of William. But the situation appears to have been rather more complex, and potentially of great interest. That William and Meurig were brothers of Philip ap Rees seems unlikely, as neither is mentioned as a potential beneficiary in the re-grant. Furthermore, the father of William and Meurig, as we shall see, appears to have been a Rees ap Meurig, which would rule them out as brothers of Rees ap Hywel ap Meurig. But there may nevertheless have been a close relationship between William and Meurig and the descendants of Hywel ap Meurig.

Meurig ap Rees occurs elsewhere in records of the period: thus in 1339 he was commissioned with Philip de Clanvowe and Adam Lucas to make inquisition regarding reported defects in Builth castle.[1] He was clearly of significance in the region around Bronllys: a charter of 1313 names him as Meurice ap Rees ap Meurice de Cantrefselyf.[2] It is just possible that he was son of the Rhys ap Meurig who witnessed, along with Hywel ap Meurig, the charter of 1271 which was given at Bronllys.[3] I have suggested that he may have been the Rhys ap Meurig who was constable of Bronllys in 1251, and that he may have been a brother of Hywel ap Meurig.[4] There are potential problems in the generation-spans implied by such an identification. Rhys ap Meurig, constable of Bronllys in 1251, cannot be identified with confidence as active any later than the early 1270s, and if he died in that period it would be unusual, though not impossible, to find a son or sons still active c.1340.[5]

In this instance, the Welsh genealogies may be of help. Tracts of seventeenth-century date, but quite possibly drawing on earlier materials, have a Meurig Ddu ap Rhys [?Rees] ap Meurig ap Rhys Gryg.[6] The descent from Rhys Gryg interestingly parallels that of Hywel ap Meurig but is rather more credible in terms of generation dates.[7] Bartrum's generation markers place Meurig as being born c.1230, therefore giving Rees/Rhys ap Meurig a birth date of c.1270, and Meurig ap Rees/Rhys one of c.1300. But those generation markers are of course somewhat artificial, and it may be necessary to move some of these dates to a rather earlier point. Rhys Gryg was active from the late twelfth century to his death in 1234. It is quite possible that we should place his birth around 1170, thus creating the possibility that a son Meurig – who, it must be stressed, does not appear in record or chronicle sources – may have had a birth date of c.1195. His son Rees/Rhys might then be born around 1225/1230, and it would not strain credibility too much to see him as the constable of Bronllys in the early 1250s. His career might then extend quite comfortably into the 1270s, and sons born in the later years of that period might survive until c.1340. The appearance of a Rhys ap Meurig as constable of Bronllys in Cantref Selyf in 1251 fits in with the fact that William and Meurig, sons of Rees ap Meurig were identified in record sources as being 'of Cantref Selyf' and with the fact that some of the descendants of Philip, son of Meurig Ddu ap Rhys/Rees, are also associated in Bartrum's pedigree with Cantref Selyf.

The possibility that there was a dynastic link between Meurig and William, sons of Rees ap Meurig and the descendants of Meurig ap Philip, is strengthened by the appearance of certain names in both pedigrees: these include Meurig, Rees/Rhys, Philip and William. The claim to descent from Rhys Gryg may hint at a common tradition with that of the descendants of Hywel ap Meurig ap Philip.

The evidence for an identification of William and Meurig sons of Rees as members of the family whose careers have been examined in this book is hardly conclusive. It is possible, but no more, that they may have been cousins of the sons of Hywel ap Meurig. But at the very least William and Meurig appear to be men of the Middle March with close associations with the descendants of Meurig ap Philip, who had also learned how to thrive in the Herefordshire March of the late thirteenth and the early fourteenth centuries. They had significant financial resources, and Meurig ap Rees, as we shall see, held a position of prominence in Cantref Selyf. It is particularly interesting that the brothers William and Meurig sons of Rees appear to have been closely involved in the development of the landholdings of the descendants of Hywel ap Meurig. We have seen how William ap Rees was central, as a feoffee, in granting to Philip ap Hywel, Rees ap Hywel and the latter's son Philip of Bronllys, with successive remainders within amongst Rees ap Hywel's descendants, the manor of Talgarth. And it has been acutely observed by Dr Wells-Furby that Meurig ap Rees, William's brother, was 'chiefly responsible for acquiring' extensive lands in Cantref Selyf, 'and from him they passed to Rees ap Howell [Hywel] of Talgarth'.[8]

It is also remarkable how William and Meurig, sons of Rees ap Meurig, stood very close to the sons of Hywel ap Meurig in the political turmoil of the early 1320s. In the period of the ascendancy of the baronial opposition to Edward II led by Thomas of Lancaster in 1321 many of those who had risen against Edward were accorded pardons at the insistence of the 'Contrariants'. One of the most prominent of the latter was the earl of Hereford and Essex, Humphrey de Bohun, a patron of the family of Hywel ap Meurig. Amongst those who received a pardon on Hereford's testimony for their actions against the king and his favourites, the Despensers, were Philip de Clanvowe, grandson of Hywel ap Meurig, and Philip ap Hywel, one of his sons. But also pardoned at the same times were Meurig ap Rees and William ap Rees.[9] By 14 February 1321/2, with the revival in Edward II's political and military fortunes, Meurig ap Rees had so far recovered his position in the eyes of the royal government that he was appointed, along with Robert de Morby, royal Keeper of the lordship of Brecon as a result of the earl's rebellion, to raise four hundred foot soldiers from the lordship, to fight against 'the Scots and the rebels'.[10] On 15 February the order went out from the chancery to restore to Meurig ap Rees his lands and goods in the lands of the castle of Bronllys and the lands of Cantref Selyf, which were in the king's hands 'for certain reasons'.[11] It is perhaps a measure of the instability and confusion in the March that on the next day, 16 February, Robert de Morby was ordered to make arrests of some twenty men in the lordship of Brecon and associated lands. The names at the head of the list are highly significant: Master Rees ap Hywel, and Philip his brother, Meurig ap Rees and William ap 'Roys' his brother. After one other name comes that of Philip de Clanvowe. There can be no better indication of the closeness, not only social but also political, between the descendants of Hywel ap Meurig and the brothers Meurig and William, sons of Rees ap Meurig.[12] It was not the last such indication: in May of 1322 orders were issued by the king for the release of certain captives from the Middle March, and prominent amongst them were Philip ap Hywel and Meurig ap Rees, whose name immediately followed Hywel's.[13] In June of the same year, in the aftermath of the king's triumph over the Contrariant lords, a commission was appointed to hear accusations that a force led by Hugh Audley the Younger, Roger Mortimer of Wigmore and Roger Mortimer of Chirk – the last two having long since surrendered and been consigned to prison – had earlier launched a destructive raid into south-east Wales. After the three lords just noted, the next names included those of Master Rees ap Hywel and Meurig ap Rees.

Following that episode, the names of Meurig ap Rees and his brother William fade significantly in the record sources. But they do re-appear in close association with Philip ap Rees in the period 1337–40.[14] The association of the two brothers and members of the dynasty of Hywel ap Meurig was undoubtedly a significant one, and points once again to the importance at a regional level of family and similar links in facilitating the rise of a Welsh gentry class in the March of Wales.

Appendix

Notes

1 *Calendar of Patent Rolls, 1338–40,* p. 284.
2 Wells-Furby, *Catalogue of the Medieval Muniments at Berkeley Castle* II, p. 364 (C2/1/2).
3 See Stephenson, 'Conquerors, courtiers, and careerists', p. 50. But a Rhys ap Meurig was the last of the witnesses to Edmund Mortimer's charter to Walter Hakelutel of 1285, for which see p. 27 above.
4 Stephenson, 'Conquerors, courtiers, and careerists', pp. 38, 41.
5 Wells-Furby, *Catalogue of the Medieval Muniments at Berkeley Castle* II, p. 666 (C2/1/13).
6 Bartrum, *Welsh Genealogies*, IV, Rhys ap Tewdwr 17.
7 For the alleged descent of Hywel ap Meurig from Rhys Gryg, see p. 6 above, and cf p. 124.
8 See Wells-Furby, *Catalogue of the Medieval Muniments at Berkeley Castle,* II, pp. 664–6. On a minor point, it is probable that some of the lands acquired by Meurig ap Rees passed from him directly to Sir Philip ap Rees [ap Hywel], as Master Rees ap Hywel died some years earlier (in 1328) than Dr Wells-Furby assumes.
9 *Calendar of Patent Rolls, 1321–24*, p. 18.
10 Ibid., p. 73.
11 *Calendar of Close Rolls, 1318–23*, p. 420.
12 *Calendar of Patent Rolls, 1321–24*, p. 77.
13 *Calendar of Close Rolls, 1318–23*, p. 458.
14 Wells-Furby, *Catalogue of the Medieval Muniments at Berkeley Castle*, II, p. 666.

Bibliography

Primary sources

Unpublished

Berkeley Castle Muniments, BCM/C/2/2/8.
London, The National Archives [TNA], E 101/3/11.
London, TNA E 101/401/16.
London, TNA E 372/126.
London, TNA, SC6/1209/9.
London, TNA, SC6/1221/3 no. 2 m. 1.
London, TNA, SC6/1221/3 m. 8.
London, TNA, SC6/1221/4 m. 4.
London, TNA C 1/16/78.
London, TNA, C 131/2/16.
London, TNA C 241/117/25.
London, TNA, CP 25/1/82/33, no. 137.
London, TNA CP 25/1/82/37, no. 7.

Printed

Bannister, A. T. (ed.), *Registrum Ade de Orleton, Episcopi Herefordensis* (London: Canterbury and York Society, 1908).
Barrow, J. S. (ed.), *Fasti Ecclesiae Anglicanae 1066–1300: vol. 8, Hereford* (London: Institute of Historical Research, 2002).
Bartrum, P. C., *Welsh Genealogies AD 300–1400* (Cardiff: University of Wales Press, 1974).
Public Record Office publications, all London: HMSO:
    Calendar of Charter Rolls, 1226–1516 (6 vols, 1903–27).
    Calendar of Close Rolls, 1272–1500 (46 vols, 1900–55).

Calendar of Fine Rolls, 1272–1471 (12 vols, 1911–49).

Calendar of Inquisitions, Miscellaneous, 1216–1377 (3 vols, 1916–37).

Calendar of Inquisitions Post Mortem (1904–).

Calendar of Patent Rolls, 1332–1509 (1906–16).

Calendar of Liberate Rolls, 1226–72 (1917–).

Calendar of Various Chancery Rolls, 1277–1326 (1912).

Close Rolls 1227–1272 (4 vols, 1902–38).

Patent Rolls 1216–32 (2 vols, 1901–03).

Register of Edward the Black Prince Part I A.D. 1346–1348 (1930).

Capes, William W. (ed.), *Registrum Ricardi de Swinfield* (London: Canterbury and York Society, 1909).

Carte, T. (ed.), *Rotuli Francie* (London, 1743).

Carte, T. (ed.), *Catalogue des Rolles Gascons, Normans et Francois II* (London, 1763).

Davies, J. C. (ed.), *The Welsh Assize Roll, 1277–84* (Cardiff: University of Wales Press, 1940).

Denholm-Young, N. (ed.), *Vita Edwardi Secundi* (London, 1957).

Edwards, J. G. (ed.), *Calendar of Ancient Correspondence concerning Wales* (Cardiff: University of Wales Press, 1935).

Edwards, J. G. (ed.), *Littere Wallie* (Cardiff: University of Wales Press, 1940).

Fryde, Natalie (ed.), *List of Welsh Entries in the Memoranda Rolls 1282–1343* (Cardiff: University of Wales Press, 1974).

Furnivall, Frederick J., *The Fifty Earliest English Wills in the Court of Probate, London, A.D. 1387–1439*, EETS [Original Series] 78 (London,1882).

Hardy, Thomas Duffus (ed.), *Rotuli Litterarum Patentium in Turri Londinensi Asservati*, vol. 1, part 1 [1201–1216] (London: Record Commission, 1835).

Horn, Joyce M. (ed.), *Fasti Ecclesiae Anglicanae 1300–1541: vol. 3, Salisbury Diocese* (London, 1962).

Inquisitions and Assessments relating to Feudal Aids, vol. 2 (London: HMSO, 1900).

Jeayes, I. H., *Descriptive Catalogue of the Charters and Muniments in the Possession of Lord Fitzhardinge at Berkeley Castle* (Bristol, 1892).

Johnstone, Hilda (ed.), *Letters of Edward of Caernarfon, 1284–1307* (Manchester: Manchester University Press, 1946).

Jones, Francis (ed.), 'The subsidy of 1292', *Bulletin of the Board of Celtic Studies*, 13 (1950).

Jones, Thomas (ed. and trans.), *Brut y Tywysogion, or The Chronicle of the Princes: Peniarth MS. 20 Version* (Cardiff: University of Wales Press, 1952).

Livingston, Michael, and John K. Bollard (eds), *Owain Glyndŵr: A Casebook* (Liverpool: Liverpool University Press, 2013).

Lumby, J. R. (ed.), *Polychronicon Ranulphi Higden* (London: Rolls Series, 9 vols, 1865–86), vol. 9.

Nicolas, Harris (ed.), *Proceedings and Ordinances of the Privy Council of England, 10 Richard II to 11 Henry IV* (London: Record Commission, 1834).

Nicolas, N. H., *Testamenta Vetusta*, vol. I (London, 1826).

Nicolas, Sir N. Harris, *The Controversy Sir Richard Scrope and Sir Robert Grosvenor in the Court of Chivalry A.D. MCCCLXXXV–MCCCLX* (London, 1832).

Original Documents produced as a supplement to the Archaeologia Cambrensis, vol. 1, 1877.

Parliamentary Writs and Writs of Military Summons.

Rees, William (ed.), *Calendar of Ancient Petitions relating to Wales* (Cardiff: University of Wales Press, 1975).

Stubbs, William (ed.), *Chronicles of the Reigns of Edward I and Edward I*, vol. II (London: Rolls Series, 1883).

Webb, John (ed.), *A Roll of the Household Expenses of Richard de Swinfield, Bishop of Hereford, 1289–90* (London: Camden Society, 1854).

Wells-Furby, Bridget (ed.), *A Catalogue of the Medieval Muniments at Berkeley Castle*, 2 vols, Gloucestershire Record Series, vol. 17 and 18 (Bristol and Gloucestershire Archaeological Society, 2004).

Williams ab Ithel, J. (ed.), *Annales Cambriae* (London: Rolls Series, 1860).

Secondary works

Alcock, L., D. J. C. King, W. G. Putnam, C. J. Spurgeon, 'Excavations at Castell Bryn Amlwg', *Montgomeryshire Collections*, 60 (1967–8), 8–27.

Banks, Lawrence, 'Three houses on one estate', *Transactions of the Radnorshire Society*, 72 (2012), 121–38.

Brooks, Alan, and Nikolaus Pevsner, *The Buildings of England: Herefordshire* (London: Yale University Press, 2012).

Burtscher, Michael, *The FitzAlans, Earls of Arundel and Surrey, Lords of the Welsh Marches (1267–1415)* (Almeley: Logaston Press, 2008).

Carr, A. D., *The Gentry of North Wales in the Later Middle Ages* (Cardiff: University of Wales Press, 2017), pp. 28–66.

Chapman, Adam, *Welsh Soldiers in the Later Middle Ages, 1282–1422* (Woodbridge: Boydell Press, 2015).

Charles, B. G., 'An early charter of the abbey of Cwmhir', *Radnorshire Society Transactions*, 40 (1970), 68–74.

Davies, J. Conway, 'The Despenser war in Glamorgan', *Transactions of the Royal Historical Society*, 3rd Series, 9 (1915), 21–64.

Davies, John, 'Owen of Montgomery: Priest, King's Clerk and Military Officer', *Montgomeryshire Collections*, 104 (2016), 17–24.

Davies, R. R., *Lordship and Society in the March of Wales, 1284–1400* (Oxford: The Clarendon Press, 1978).

Davies, R. R., The Age of Conquest: Wales 1063–1415 (Oxford: Oxford University Press, 2000).

Deanesly, Margaret, *The Lollard Bible* (Cambridge: Cambridge University Press, 1920).

Denholm-Young, N., *History and Heraldry 1254–1310* (Oxford: The Clarendon Press, 1965).

Düll, Siegrid, A. Luttrell and Maurice Keen, 'Faithful unto death: the tomb slab of Sir William Neville and Sir John Clanvowe, Constantinople 1391', *Antiquaries Journal*, 71 (1991), 174–90.

Edwards, J. G., 'The treason of Thomas Turberville', in R. W. Hunt et al. (eds), *Studies in Medieval History presented to Frederick Maurice Powicke* (Oxford: The Clarendon Press, 1948), pp. 296–309.

Eyton, R. W., *Antiquities of Shropshire*, IV (London, 1857).

Griffiths, Ralph A., *Conquerors and Conquered in Medieval Wales* (Stroud: Alan Sutton, 1994).

Griffiths, Ralph A., 'Owain Glyn Dŵr's invasion of the central March of Wales in 1402: the evidence of clerical taxation', *Studia Celtica*, 46 (2012), 111–22.

Griffiths, Ralph A., *The Principality of Wales in the Late Middle Ages: The Structure and Personnel of Government. I, South Wales 1277–1536* (Cardiff: University of Wales Press, 1972).

Haines, Roy Martin, *King Edward II: His Life, His Reign, and its Aftermath, 1284–1330* (Montreal: McGill-Queen's University Press, 2003).

Holden, Brock, *Lords of the Central Marches: English Aristocracy and Frontier Society 1087–1265* (Oxford: Oxford University Press, 2008).

Holmes, G. A., *The Estates of the Higher Nobility in Fourteenth-Century England* (Cambridge: Cambridge University Press, 1957).

Hopkinson, Charles, and Martin Speight, *The Mortimers, Lords of the March* (Almeley: Logaston Press, 2002).

Jones, B. (ed.), *Fasti Ecclesiae Anglicanae 1300–1541: Volume 11, the Welsh Dioceses (Bangor, Llandaff, St Asaph, St Davids)* (London: Institute of Historical Research, 1965).

Jones, Craig Owen, *Llywelyn Bren* (Llanrwst: Gwasg Carreg Gwalch, 2006).

Jones, Craig Owen, *The Revolt of Madog ap Llywelyn* (Pwllheli: Llygad Gwalch, 2008).

Jones, Emrys (ed.), *The Welsh in London 1500–2000* (Cardiff: University of Wales Press on behalf of The Honourable Society of Cymmrodorion, 2001).

Jones, M., *Ducal Brittany, 1364–1399* (Oxford: Oxford University Press, 1970).

Jones, M. C., *The Feudal Barons of Powys* (London, 1868).

Kightly, Charles, 'Clanvowe, Thomas (d. 1410) of Hergest and Yazor, Herefs', in J. S. Roskill, L. Clark and C. Rawcliffe (eds), *The History of Parliament: The House of Commons 1386–1421* (Woodbridge: Boydell and Brewer, 1993); this can be consulted online, at *https://www.historyofparliamentonline.org/volume/1386-1421/member/clanvowe-thomas-1410* (accessed 16 August 2020).

Kittredge, G. L., 'Chaucer and some of his friends', *Modern Philology*, 1 (June 1903) 1–18.

Lieberman, Max, *The March of Wales 1067–1300* (Cardiff: University of Wales Press, 2008).

Lieberman, Max, *The Medieval March of Wales: The Creation and Perception of a Frontier, 1066–1283* (Cambridge: Cambridge University Press, 2010).

Lloyd, J. E., *Owen Glendower* (Oxford: The Clarendon Press, 1931).

Maddicott, J. R., *Simon de Montfort* (Cambridge: Cambridge University Press, 1994).

McColly, William, 'The "Book of Cupid" as an Imitation of Chaucer: a Stylo-Statistical View', *The Chaucer Review*, 18/3 (Winter 1984), 239–49.

McFarlane, K. B., *Lancastrian Kings and Lollard Knights* (Oxford: The Clarendon Press, 1972).

Morgan, Richard, 'An extent of the lordship of Hay', *Brycheiniog*, 28 (1995–96), 15–21.

Phillips, Seymour, *Edward II* (London: Yale University Press, 2011).

Powell, A. D., 'The Clanvowes', *Transactions of the Radnorshire Society*, 58 (1988), 21–4.

Roskell, J. S., L. Clark and C. Rawcliffe (eds), *The History of Parliament: The House of Commons 1386–1421* (Woodbridge: Boydell and Brewer, 1993); particularly relevant entries by Charles Kightly can be consulted online at: *https://www.historyofparliamentonline.org/volume/1386-1421/ member/clanvowe-thomas-1410*; *https://www.historyofparliamentonline.org/ volume/1386-1421/member/whitney-sir-robert-i-1402*.

Scattergood, John, 'The date of Sir John Clanvowe's "The Two Ways" and the "Reinvention of Lollardy", *Medium Aevum*, 79/1 (2010), 116–20.

Scourfield, Robert, and Richard Haslam, *The Buildings of Wales: Powys* (London: Yale University Press, 2013).

Seaton, Ethel, *Sir Richard Roos* (London, 1961).

Seymour, M. C., 'Sir John Clanvowe 1341–1391', *Transactions of the Radnorshire Society*, 75 (2005), 35–58.

Siddons, Michael Powell, *The Development of Welsh Heraldry* II (Aberystwyth: National Library of Wales, 1993).

Skeat, W. W., *The Chaucer Canon* (Oxford: The Clarendon Press, 1900).

Smith, J. Beverley, 'Edward II and the allegiance of Wales', *Welsh History Review*, 8 (1976–7), 139–71.

Smith, J. Beverley, 'Gruffudd Llwyd and the Celtic Alliance', *BBCS*, 26 (1974–6), 463–78.

Smith, J. Beverley, 'Marcher regality: Quo Warranto proceedings relating to Cantrefselyf in the lordship of Brecon, 1349', *BBCS*, 28 (1978–80), 267–88.

Smith, J. Beverley, 'The Middle March in the Thirteenth century', *Bulletin of the Board of Celtic Studies*, 24 (1970), 77–94.

Stephenson, David, 'A treaty too far? The impact of the treaty of Montgomery on Llywelyn ap Gruffudd's principality of Wales', *Montgomeryshire Collections*, 106 (2018), 19–32.

Stephenson, David, 'Conquerors, courtiers and careerists: the struggle for supremacy in Brycheiniog, 1093–1282', *Brycheiniog*, 44 (2013), 27–51.

Stephenson, David, 'Crisis and Continuity in a Fourteenth-Century Welsh Lordship: The Struggle for Powys, 1312–32', *Cambrian Medieval Celtic Studies* (2013), 57–78.

Stephenson, David, 'Empires in Wales: from Gruffudd ap Llywelyn to Llywelyn ap Gruffudd', *Welsh History Review*, 28/1 (2016), 29–54.

Stephenson, David, *Medieval Powys: Kingdom, Principality and Lordships, 1132–1293* (Woodbridge: Boydell Press, 2016).

Stephenson, David, *Medieval Wales c.1050–1332: Centuries of Ambiguity* (Cardiff: University of Wales Press, 2019).

Stephenson, David, 'New light on a dark deed: the death of Llywelyn ap Gruffudd, prince of Wales', *Archaeologia Cambrensis*, 166 (2017), 243–52.

Stephenson, David, *Political Power in Medieval Gwynedd: Governance and the Welsh Princes* (Cardiff: University of Wales Press, 2014).

Stephenson, David, 'Seals in medieval Wales', *Archaeologia Cambrensis*, 166 (2017), 323–31.

Stephenson, David, 'The Chronicler of Cwm-hir Abbey, 1257–63: The Construction of a Welsh Chronicle', in R. A. Griffiths and P. R. Schofield (eds), *Wales and the Welsh in the Middle Ages* (Cardiff: University of Wales Press, 2011).

Symons, Dana, (ed.), *Chaucerian Dream Visions and Complaints* (Kalamazoo: Teams Middle English Texts, 2004). See also *https://d.lib.rochester.edu/teams/text/symons-chaucerian-dream-visions-and-complaints-boke-of-cupide-introduction*. For the edited text, see *https://d.lib.rochester.edu/teams/text/symons-chaucerian-dream-visions-and-complaints-boke-of-cupide*.

Tout, T. F., *Chapters in the Administrative History of Medieval England IV* (Manchester: Manchester University Press, 1928).

Unpublished theses

Davies, R. R., 'The Bohun and Lancaster Lordships in Wales in the Fourteenth and early Fifteenth Centuries' (unpublished D.Phil. thesis, University of Oxford, 1965).

Kightly, Charles, 'The Early Lollards' (unpublished Ph.D. thesis, York University, 1975).

Index

A

Abergavenny 7, 46 n.5, 91
Almeley 112
Anne of Bohemia, Queen 83, 88, 96, 101
Arundel, earl of 35, 43, 56, 70–1, 77 n.12, 91, 113, 120 n.22
Aston, Sir John 120 n.20
Audley, Hugh 126
Audley, Nicholas 84, 103 n.20

B

Bagot, William 38
Baldock, Robert 56
Bannockburn, battle of 38
Baskerville, Richard de 41, 48 n.41, 113, 120 n.20
Beauchamp, Sir William, lord of Abergavenny 86, 91–2, 105 n.53, 106 nn.56 and 65
Bere, Sir Kynard de la 93–4, 106 n.66
Bishampton 112
Black Death x, 81
Blaenllyfni 36, 54, 56, 59–61, 72, 79 n.46
Bluet, Elizabeth 63–4, 116, 118
Bluet, John 63
Bluet, Ralph 116

Blunt, Thomas le 77 n.10
Bohun, Humphrey de, earl of Hereford, lord of Brecon (d. 1275) 14, 18
Bohun, Humphrey de, Junior (d. 1265) 2, 29 n.11
Bohun, Humphrey de, Junior (d. 1298) 14, 19, 29 n.11, 33, 35
Bohun, Humphrey de, Junior (d. 1322) 40–2, 51–2, 54, 56, 60, 70, 125
Bohun, Humphrey de, Junior (d. 1361) 61, 118
Bohun, Humphrey de, Junior (d. 1373) 82, 90, 10, 102 n.9
Bohun, John de, earl of Hereford, lord of Brecon (d. 1336) 77 n.12, 57
Bohun, William de, earl of Northampton 62–3, 118
Book of Cupid (*The Cuckoo and the Nightingale*) 86–8, 104 nn.30 and 35
Boroughbridge, battle of 41, 56, 70–1
Bradestan, Sir Thomas de 73–4
Braose, William de (d. 1211) 8
Braose, William de (d. 1230) 7
Braose, William de, lord of Gower (d. 1326) 53

Bray, Henry de 18, 22–3
Brecknock 54
Brecon, archdeacon of 28, 44–5, 115
Brecon, lordship of 14–15, 29 n.11,
    33–5, 41, 48 n.44, 56, 60, 62,
    126
Bredwardine, family of 78 n.42
Bret, Philip le 11–12
Brinsop 79 n.46
Brittany, John, duke of 85
Brompton, Brian de 11
Bronllys, castle and lordship of 15–16,
    54, 56, 59–60, 62–4, 118, 124,
    126
Bronllys, Elizabeth de 66 n.31, 123
Bronllys, James de 66 n.31, 123
Bronllys, John de 65 n.31, 123
Bronllys, Philip de 58–64, 65 n.31,
    66 n.34, 69, 116, 123, 125
Bronllys, Rees de 66 n.31
Bruce, Edward 38–9, 52
Brut, Walter 95
Bryn Amlwg, castle 17, 30 n.24
Bryn Glas, battle of 94
Builth castle 22–4, 26, 31n 60, 36,
    37–8, 47 n.30, 54, 56, 60, 71,
    79 n.46, 96–7, 121 n.27
Builth, dean of 23-4, 27
Builth, lordship of 19, 21–3, 25–7,
    31 n.60, 47n 30, 54, 56, 60, 71,
    96–7
Burghill 79 n.46, 111–12
Burghill, Andrew of 112
Burghill, Henry of, 112
Burghill, John of 112
Burghill, Roger of 112
Burghill, Walter of 112
Butler, William le, lord of Wem
    38
Bwlchydinas 54, 60, 72, 79 n.46

C
Caldecot 36–7, 52
Cantref Selyf 14–15, 54, 56, 59–63,
    66 n.38, 118, 124–6
Carles, Roger 42
Castile 82
Cedewain 17, 54
Cefnllys castle 2, 5–6, 12–14, 16, 54
Cefn Rhosferig 23–4
Celtic alliance, the 38, 47 n.32
Ceri [Kerry] 54
Chastel Goodrich, Thomas du 74
Chaucer, Geoffrey x, 86–8
Chaumpaigne, Cecily 86
Cheyne, Sir John 92
Chirbury 38
Clanvowe, John (d. c.1361) 81–2
Clanvowe, Sir John, 82–92 passim,
    95, 97, 103 nn.18 and 25, 104
    nn.28, 30 and 42, 105 n.45. 106
    nn.65 and 66
Clanvowe, Perryne see Whitney, Perryne
Clanvowe, Sir Philip de 70–9 passim,
    112–16, 119–20, 123
Clanvowe, Thomas 82
Clanvowe, Sir Thomas 92–8 passim
Clare, Gilbert de, earl of Gloucester
    34, 52, 54
Clement, Robert 72
Clifford lords 15–16, 30 n.21
Clifford, Sir Lewis 89, 92, 105 n.45
Clun 17–18
Constantinople 85
Corbet, Peter de 71
Corbet, Thomas 11
Cradock, David 83
Crickhowell 54
Croft, Hugh de 37
Croft, John 95
Cusop 75, 113, 118, 121 n.29

Index

D

Despenser, Hugh the Elder 40–1, 43–4, 53, 70
Despenser, Hugh the Younger 40–1, 43–4, 53, 56, 70
Devereux, Walter 92, 106 n.55, 115
Dinboeth castle 54
Dolsuleyn 75, 113
Dore abbey 15–16, 19
Dover castle 55
Dryslwyn castle 33

E

Edmund of Lancaster 18–19
Ednyfed Fychan 12, 21, 29 n.6
descendants of 12, 21–2, 52, 110
Edward I 17–24, 33–4, 51
Edward II (Edward of Caernarfon) x, 38, 42, 44, 55–6, 58, 66 n.54, 70, 123, 125
Edward III 56, 60, 81–2, 91, 115
Edward the Black Prince 61, 73, 117, 122 n.32
Einion ap Madog 18–19, 23–4, 27
Einion Sais 48 n.44, 119 n.1
Elfael Is Mynydd 18, 30 n.29
Elfael Uwch Mynydd 19, 27, 31 n.69
Elizabeth de Bronllys, daughter of Philip ap Rees 63–4, 116
Elizabeth de Bronllys, daughter of Sir Philip Clanvowe 116
Elizabeth de Bronllys, daughter of Rees ap Hywel 58, 66, 123
Elizabeth de Bronllys, daughter of Rees ap Rees 64, 116, 118
Ewyas Harold 92, 106 n.56
Eylesford, Gerard of 112

F

Famine, the Great (1315–22) x
Finsbury, prebend of 56

FitzAlan, Edmund, earl of Arundel 57, 77 n.12
Alice, daughter of 77 n.12
Fitz Reginald, John 37, 58
Flanders, 1339 expedition to 72–3
Flanders, 1390 embassy to 85
Fowey, theft of ship at 73
Fremingham, Ralph de 20–1

G

Gamage, Elizabeth 112
Gentry, English 59, 76
Herefordshire 93, 101, 117
of the March ix, 63, 126
Welsh xi, 110
Giffard, John 15, 18, 59
Giffard, Maud 59
Gladestry, manor of 7–8, 15, 75, 102 n.5, 106 n.70, 111
Glamorgan, Despenser war in 40
Glyn Dŵr, Owain 93–5, 98, 100–1, 115, 117, 119
Goronwy ap Heilyn 20–1
Gower, land of 53, 56, 59
Grandison, Peter de 79 n.46
Grey, John de 39, 47 n.34
Grey, Reginald, lord of Ruthin 94
Gruffudd ap Cliffo 30 n.21
Gruffudd Fychan (de la Pole) 38
Gruffudd Llwyd, Sir, (Gruffudd ap Rhys) 39, 52, 54, 110

H

Hakelutel, Walter 27, 36–7, 60
Hanmer, David 83
Havard, Philip and John 41, 48 n.41
Henry III 1, 5–6, 12–13, 114
Hereford 35, 43, 55, 74, 102, 111–12, 117, 121 n.22
cathedral 44, 75, 115
diocese 44–5, 51, 111

Herefordshire x, 14, 26, 31 n.61, 35,
    44–5, 59, 70, 74–6, 81–3, 90–3,
    95, 97–8, 100–2, 106 nn. 55
    and 65, 107 n.87, 109, 111–15,
    117–19, 125
Hergest 14–15, 35, 44, 51, 75, 90,
    95–7, 102, 111, 113, 118, 121
    n.31
Hinckley, Sir John 43–4, 48 n.49
Hopton, Walter de 20–2
Hore, Master William 52
Hothum, John de 40
Hywel ap Hywel 48 n.44
Hywel ap Meurig 2, 5–9, 11–27
    passim, 29 n.4, 30 n.30, 31 nn.
    44 and 59, 35, 41, 45, 46 n.9,
    48 n.44, 64, 67 n.57, 72, 76,
    90, 95–6, 101, 110–11, 114–16,
    118–19, 123–6

I

Ieuan ap Rhys 7
Ieuan ap Rees 60
Ifor ap Gruffudd 18–19
Isabella, Queen (m. Edward II) 43, 55
Isabella, Queen (m. Richard II) 92–3
Is Cennen 91

J

Joan, late wife of John Wake 37
Joan, wife of Philip ap Rees 62–3, 116
John, King 8
John ap Hywel ap Meurig 23, 30 n.30
John le Receiver 48 n.41

K

Kent, Joan of 89, 105 n.46
Kinardesle, Simon de 77 n.10
King's Pyon 75, 112–13, 120 n.13
    121 n.31

Kington 35, 51, 121 n.31
Kinnerley 66 n.37
Knovill, Bogo de 23

L

Lancaster, Thomas earl of 41, 43,
    115, 125
Lawrence, John 84
Leighton (Herefordshire) 112
Lestrange, Margaret 21
Leulingham, truce of 85
Lingayne, John de 11–13
Lollardy x, 89, 95, 101, 105 nn.42
    and 45, 107 n.92
London, Tower of 20, 41–2, 55
Lords Appellant 90
Lucas, Adam 7, 72, 74, 76, 79 n.46
    123
Lynde, Richard de la 59, 112
Lyra, abbot of 112

Ll

Llanbadarn Fawr (Ceredigion) 22, 73
Llantrisant 56
Lleucu, wife of Einion ap Madog 24,
    27
Llywelyn ap Gruffudd, prince of
    Wales 1–2, 5, 12–13, 15–17,
    19, 21, 25, 110–11
Llywelyn ap Gruffudd of
    Senghennydd (Llywelyn Bren)
    40, 52
Llywelyn ap Caradog 16, 19
Llywenny 76, 113

M

Mabel, daughter of Philip ap Rees 64,
    116
Maelienydd 2, 8, 12, 17–18, 35, 54,
    94

March of Wales ix–xi and *passim*
Martyn, William 38–9
Matilda, wife of Hywel ap Meurig
    26, 116
Matilda, wife of John Clanvowe 82
Merciless Parliament 90
Mershton, John de 7, 79 n.4
Meurice ap Rees ap Meurice 124
Meurig ap Gruffudd 15–16, 19
Meurig ap Philip xi, 7–9, 9 n.13, 12,
    59, 109–11, 116, 118, 125
Michaelchurch-on-Arrow 75, 82,
    112–13
Moles, Roger de 22
Montague, Sir John 91–2, 105 n.45
Montague, William, earl of Salisbury
    91
Montgomery 38, 57
    treaty of 15
Morby, Robert de 41, 126
Morel, Richard 86
Mortimer, Edmund (d. 1304) 7, 27,
    35, 37
Mortimer, Edmund (d. 1409) 93–4
Mortimer, Henry, of Chelmarsh 64,
    116
Mortimer, Maud (1301) 16
Mortimer, Ralph (d. 1246) 8, 11
Mortimer, Roger, of Wigmore
    (d. 1282) 1, 5–6, 10 n.14,
    11–20
Mortimer, Roger of Chirk (d. 1226)
    37, 41, 53–5, 126
Mortimer, Roger of Wigmore, earl
    of March (d. 1330) 37, 40–4,
    52, 54–5, 57, 60, 65 n.27, 121
    n.22, 126
Mortimer, Roger of Wigmore,
    2nd earl of March (d. 1360)
    102 n.5

N
Neath abbey 56
Neville, Sir William 84–6, 89, 91–2,
    103 n.12, 103 n.25, 105 n.53
Newcastle 71
Newcastle (Emlyn) 72

O
Ocle Pychard 78 n.41, 99, 111–13
Oldcastle, Sir John 95
Orwell 85
Owain ap Gruffudd ap Gwenwynwyn
    42

P
Parpoint, Philip and John 41
Partrich, Roger 96, 107 n.77
Pauncefoot, Emery 54, 77 n.10
Peasants' Revolt 83
Peasenhall, Adam de 64, 116
Pederton, Walter de 36, 51–2
Pencelli 54, 63
Penebrugg (Pembridge), Richard de
    77 n.10
Percy, Henry 84
Philip ap Hywel 7, 26, 33–49 *passim*,
    51–2, 58, 66 n.34, 69–70, 75–6,
    111–13, 115, 120 n.13, 123,
    125–6
Philip ap Rees ap Hywel 59–64, 65
    n.31, 67 n.57, 69, 111, 116,
    118, 123, 126, 127 n.8
Philpot, John 86
Pilleth, battle of 94, 101, 117
Poleyne, John 36
Pontesbury 44, 49 n.51, 58, 66 n.34
Pool castle 42–4
Pore caitif 101, 107 n.92
Poyntz, Sir John 116
Prague 83, 85, 88

Pychard, Joan 59, 112
Pychard, Miles 41, 61
Pychard, Roger 72, 77 n.10

R
Radnor 7–8, 60, 67 n.42, 75
Reading, Simon 56
Rees ap Hywel ap Meurig, Master
  27–8, 37, 39, 47 n.40, 49 n.51,
  51–9, 66 n.34, 70, 110, 114,
  116, 124–6, 127 n.8

Rh
Rhys ap Gruffudd, Sir 56, 60–1, 72,
  110, 119–20 n.3
Rhys ap Meurig 16, 124, 127 n.3
Rhys Gryg ab Yr Arglwydd Rhys 6,
  124–5, 127 n.7

S
St Davids, see of 28, 43–5, 57, 71,
  73, 115
Sapy, John de 37
Sapy, Robert de 77 n.10
Scrope v Grosvenor case 91
Scudamore, Sir John 92, 101, 106
  n.55, 107 n.87
Segrave, Hugh de 83, 91
Shaldeford, Henry 117, 121 n.32
Shifnal 62–4, 118
Shipton 56
Stanford Faucon 112
Strata Florida 2, 22
Staunton 112
Sturry, Sir Richard 89, 92, 105 n.45

T
Talbot, Gilbert 72, 74, 76, 78 n.43
Talbot, Master Philip 49 n.54
Talbot, Philippa 76

Talbot, Sir Richard 78 n.43
Three Castles, lordship of 19, 24, 30
  n.30
Tillington 112
Traveley, Walter de 15–16
Tudur ab Ednyfed 12–13
Tunis, crusade against 85
Tyrel, Hugh 7, 60, 67 n.42, 72, 75,
  79 n.46

U
Upavon 103 n.9
Usk 54, 56, 59

V
Vache, Sir Philip de la 92

W
Waldeboef, William 77 n.10
Walsingham, Thomas 89, 92, 105
  n.45
Walter ap Rhys 30 n.21
Walwayn, John 39, 41, 52
Whitney, Perryne 67 n.57, 88, 92,
  96–8, 100–2, 108 nn.100 and
  102, 116–17, 119
Whitney, Sir Robert 92–4, 96–7, 101,
  117
William ap Hywel ap Meurig 19,
  23–4, 26–8, 64, 69, 110, 112,
  115, 116
Wrottesley, Hugh 64, 116
Wycliffe, John 89, 101

Y
Yazor 75–6, 94, 97, 112–14, 118, 120
  n.20, 121 n.30
Ystrad Yw 54
Young, Hugh 83
Yweyn (alias Inge) John 53